The Real Is Radical

ALSO AVAILABLE FROM BLOOMSBURY

Laruelle and Art: The Aesthetics of Non-Philosophy, Jonathan Fardy

Capitalism's Holocaust of Animals: A Non-Marxist Critique of Capital, Philosophy and Patriarchy, Katerina Kolozova

Aesthetic Marx, ed. Samir Gandesha and Johan F. Hartle

The Real Is Radical

Marx after Laruelle

JONATHAN FARDY

BLOOMSBURY ACADEMIC
LONDON • NEW YORK • OXFORD • NEW DELHI • SYDNEY

BLOOMSBURY ACADEMIC
Bloomsbury Publishing Plc
50 Bedford Square, London, WC1B 3DP, UK
1385 Broadway, New York, NY 10018, USA
29 Earlsfort Terrace, Dublin 2, Ireland

BLOOMSBURY, BLOOMSBURY ACADEMIC and the Diana logo
are trademarks of Bloomsbury Publishing Plc

First published in Great Britain 2022
This paperback edition published 2023

Copyright © Jonathan Fardy, 2022

Jonathan Fardy has asserted his right under the Copyright, Designs and
Patents Act, 1988, to be identified as Author of this work.

For legal purposes the Acknowledgments on p. viii constitute an
extension of this copyright page.

Cover image: Full Frame Shot of Wall
(© Daniel Kaesler / EyeEm / Getty Images)

All rights reserved. No part of this publication may be reproduced or
transmitted in any form or by any means, electronic or mechanical, including
photocopying, recording, or any information storage or retrieval system,
without prior permission in writing from the publishers.

Bloomsbury Publishing Plc does not have any control over, or
responsibility for, any third-party websites referred to or in this book. All
internet addresses given in this book were correct at the time of going to
press. The author and publisher regret any inconvenience caused if addresses
have changed or sites have ceased to exist, but can accept no responsibility
for any such changes.

A catalogue record for this book is available from the British Library.

Library of Congress Cataloging-in-Publication Data

Names: Fardy, Jonathan, author.
Title: The real is radical: Marx after Laruelle / Jonathan Fardy.
Description: London; New York: Bloomsbury Academic, 2021. |
Includes bibliographical references and index. |
Identifiers: LCCN 2021006818 (print) | LCCN 2021006819 (ebook) |
ISBN 9781350168077 (hb) | ISBN 9781350168084 (epdf) |
ISBN 9781350168091 (ebook)
Subjects: LCSH: Laruelle, François. | Marx, Karl, 1818-1883. |
Socialism–History. | Radicalism–History. | Radicalism–Philosophy.
Classification: LCC HX73.F37 2021 (print) |
LCC HX73 (ebook) | DDC 335.4/1–dc23
LC record available at https://lccn.loc.gov/2021006818
LC ebook record available at https://lccn.loc.gov/2021006819

ISBN: HB: 978-1-3501-6807-7
PB: 978-1-3502-6101-3
ePDF: 978-1-3501-6808-4
eBook: 978-1-3501-6809-1

Typeset by Integra Software Services Pvt. Ltd.

To find out more about our authors and books visit
www.bloomsbury.com and sign up for our newsletters.

For my son, Elijah: your realness is so radical.

CONTENTS

Acknowledgments viii

1 Introduction 1
2 Stranger 15
3 Struggle 49
4 Impossibilization 95
5 Fiction 131
6 Metaphysics 169
7 Conclusion 195

Notes 200

Index 217

ACKNOWLEDGMENTS

I want to thank the many wonderful scholars and translators of Laruelle's work: Taylor Adkins, Katerina Kolozova, Anthony Paul Smith, Drew S. Burk, Rocco Gangle, John O'Maoilearca, Ian James, and many others. Your work has been foundational for me. I also want to thank my editors, Liza Thompson and Dr. Lucy Russell at Bloomsbury Academic. I want to thank my family: Lisa, Jim, Mom and Dad. I want to say "I love you" to Elijah. Finally, thank you to Amy Wuest, PhD, who remains my most trusted partner in all things Real and philosophical.

1

Introduction

This book is centrally concerned with explicating and developing François Laruelle's "non-standard" approach to Marx and Marxism or what he calls "non-Marxism." Laruelle's non-Marxist project dovetails with his larger intellectual project of "non-standard philosophy" or "non-philosophy."[1] In this introductory chapter, I cover the basics of non-philosophy, clarify my method, and provide a brief outline of the chapters to follow.

Basics of Non-Philosophy

It is an irony of history that one of the most theoretically sophisticated and inventive ripostes to the Marxist tradition is so often confused with its negation. Non-Marxism is Laruelle's non-philosophical political project. Non-philosophy is a way of doing philosophy that refuses to decide on what Laruelle simply calls the "Real." Laruelle identifies this decision on the Real—what Laruelle calls "Philosophical Decision"—as the invariant gesture of "standard philosophy." Let me clarify these notions as they are central to what follows.

Laruelle holds that standard philosophy is fundamentally structured by what he calls *Philosophical Decision on the Real*. This gesture of decision has taken a host of forms. These include, for example, Plato's "Forms," Descartes's "cogito," Kant's "noumena," Hegel's "absolute," Schopenhauer's "will," Heidegger's "Being," Derrida's "*différance*," Deleuze and Guattari's "plane of immanence," and many more. Such philosophical decisions order a set of concepts and determine the structure of a philosophical program. Laruelle rejects the decisionist imperative of standard philosophy. For Laruelle, the Real cannot be decided by thought for the Real is precisely what determines the possibility of thought itself. The Real is the radical immanence of which thought is a part. But there is no vantage in the Real by which thought could enter into a relation of exchange or equivalence with the Real. Thought is *in* but never *on* the Real. Non-philosophy opposes Philosophical Decision on the grounds that it is a mere pretension that any philosophy has sufficient resources or the requisite perspective to capture the Real in concepts. This pretension of standard philosophy—what Laruelle calls the "Principle of Standard Philosophy"—stymies standard philosophy's capacity for self-criticism. "The other side of this pretension," notes Laruelle, "is the impossibility of philosophy being a rigorous thinking of itself."[2] Standard philosophy claims to decide on what is decisive for its existence and thus cannot think its own finitude. The Real is decisive for thought—philosophical and non-philosophical—but only, as Laruelle consistently reminds us, "in-the-last-instance." This concept of "the-last-instance" is cloned from the work of Louis Althusser, who himself took it from Friedrich Engels. The latter famously noted that he and Marx only ever held that the economy was decisive for historical and political change *in the last instance*. Althusser theoretically radicalized this claim via his concept of "overdetermination," which names for Althusser a basic fact of historical change, namely, that every change is determined by a multiplicity of factors such that it is irresponsible, if not impossible, to credit any one factor as determinant. Althusser extends the critique of "economism" inaugurated by Engels and Marx, but adds the caveat that even the "last instance" of the economy "never comes."[3]

Laruelle in turn radicalizes Althusser's concept of overdetermination and applies it to the Real. It is the Real for Laruelle that is determinant but only in the last instance, but this last instance is never (and never can be) an instance for Philosophical Decision. What appears as such from the standpoint of Philosophical Decision is the chimera of philosophy. Now, it is important here to add that non-philosophy's insistence that the Real cannot be decided except by philosophical self-delusion does not mean that there is no Real or no reality. Quite the opposite is the case. Non-philosophy axiomatically posits the Real as foreclosed to philosophical reason. Yet at the same time the Real is axiomatically held to be determinant in the last instance. The Real then is determinant but does not "relate" to philosophy. Laruelle terms this non-relationality of the Real "unilateral duality." The Real is axiomatically nominated as "One-in-One" and held to be determinative for the possibility of philosophy—and even its pseudo-decisionist dynamic—but it is not a "oneness" that philosophical material *relates to* because it is part of the Real in the last instance, even though this "last instance" never arrives as a subject for philosophical reason. Laruelle writes:

> Non-philosophy, precisely in reducing the Real to its solitude of One-in-One, without logical determination … opens up the possibility of the manifestation of a non(-One), of an empirical there is which is now that of philosophy itself, of the World, Being, Logic, etc. In effect, if the One is absolutely indifferent, it no longer negates and can leave thought (as organon rather than ready-made or fetishized thought) to validate this resistance within certain limits or give it its "true" object … [which] needs this resistance in order to constitute the order of non-philosophy and its statements.[4]

Non-philosophy doesn't just leave the Real to itself. It axiomatically holds that the Real is whether or not philosophy decides its nature or decides to leave it alone. This axiomatization of the Real's "solitude"—written as "One-in-One"—releases standard philosophy *qua* "non (-One)" (written as such to denote its pseudo-break with the Real) from its relationality to the Real by axiomatically affirming its material determination by the Real. The Real is indifferent and thus it does not "negate" thought. Standard philosophical thought is defetishized precisely insofar as its fetishized exchange-claim on the Real is formally voided. Philosophy ceases to be a fetishized decisionist dynamic and is instead reorganized as an "organon"—literally an "instrument" or "means" for thought—rather than standard philosophy's reified self-projection of legitimate thought itself. Philosophy *qua* "organon" becomes an instrument that self-validates no longer its exchange-claim on the Real. Rather, philosophy's self-generated (if denied) resistance or friction between concept and Real becomes, from the standpoint of non-philosophy, philosophy's "true object." The "resistance" or friction between concept and Real is no longer treated as a problem to be overcome but is rather non-philosophy's point of departure: this resistance "constitutes the order of non-philosophy and its statements." *I take this "resistance" to be formally a non-capitalist practice of thought insofar as it validates the resistance and thus non-equivalence and non-exchangeability between philosophical reason and the Real.*

The axiom of unilateral duality conditions the non-philosophical possibility of rendering standard philosophical materials as raw materials precisely by rewriting them not as signs referring to the Real, but rather, as Rocco Gangle notes, in such a way that "conceptual material becomes an algebraic sign available for purely formal operations."[5] This non-philosophical formalism is entirely different from standard philosophical formalism precisely because it is syntactically formatted to formally break the delusional law of *thought-for-the-Real* immanent to philosophical reason. But—and this is key— the "algebraic" form of non-philosophy is not an *empty formalism* precisely because in its unilaterality it "clones" (Laruelle's term) the actual relation of non-relationality to the Real. Insofar as "philosophical terms are converted essentially into variables," writes Gangle, "for possible substitutions that are purely operational and equational in nature," then non-philosophical algebraic syntax remains formally subordinate to the determinant non-substitutability of the algebraic sign of the Real. Non-philosophy enables philosophical concepts to become *material* precisely because its formalist procedure treats them as *whatever material*. All philosophical material is "equal" according to non-philosophical formalism by reason of its non-equivalence and non-exchangeability for the Real. But this formalism and formal equality *does not treat all material as equal in its own right*. Non-philosophy recognizes important differences between philosophical materials but it recognizes no difference in terms of their relation to the Real. Gangle explains this very well in the simplest algebraic terms: Let Real be designated as "X" and let philosophy be designated as "Y." "X" determines the possibility of "Y" in a unilateral manner. But "X" is not in a bidirectional "relation" with "Y." The algebraic relation is not bivalent. "X" is a function of "Y." But "Y" is not a function of "X." "X" is determined by "Y" but "X" does not determine "Y." Hence, non-philosophy proceeds axiomatically by "positing the One as the radically immanent Real."[6] But this "One" is not that of monism, onto-theology, or any other *philosophical* concept of unity. The oneness of the Real cannot be thought otherwise than axiomatically because our inherited logics and languages are deeply dualistic. Non-philosophy works with this dualistic inheritance but voids it of its ontological pretensions. The "style of philosophy," notes Laruelle, demands that we "treat everything through a duality (of problems) that does not form *a* Two as a set, and through an identity (of problems, and thus solutions) that does not form a Unity or synthesis."[7] Non-philosophy "is presented as an immanent thought," notes John O'Maoilearca, "precisely *because* it does not try to think the Real but only alongside or 'according to' it."[8]

Non-Marxism extends the non-philosophical project in a Marxian political direction. It is firstly a critique of the imbrication of philosophy and capital. Both systems function by trading signs for the Real. Philosophy and capitalism function according to the intertwined logics of equivalence and exchange. Capitalism axiomatically assumes that things can always be exchanged for their equivalent in value. Philosophy likewise axiomatically assumes that the Real can be exchanged for its equivalence in concepts. Laruelle terms the shared logic of capitalism and philosophy "supercapitalism." "Supercapitalism is the philosophy-form" that defines the "global functioning of societies."[9] Non-Marxism treats the Marxist philosophical tradition as *conceptual raw materials* for thinking against the standard philosophical logic of exchange and equivalence through a theoretical resistance to supercapitalist logic.

Marxism has historically been treated as a *philosophical problem* in part because the multiplicity of its postures is a problem for philosophers who want to find in Marxism (or force upon it) a singular and unified *philosophical* identity. "The multiplicity of the 'sources' of Marxism, and first of Marx's thought itself," writes Laruelle, presents itself to philosophers as a "seemingly 'baroque' character … which philosophers hesitate before."[10] Philosophical responses to Marx's work and to the Marxist tradition have frequently taken the form of rescue operations and cleanup jobs. Philosophers interpret Marx and Marxism "as a deficient organization," writes Laruelle, "to be reorganized on the basis of some new or old ontological postulates imported into the [Marxist] edifice."[11] This approach can never make good on its promises. It merely has the effect of fragmenting the Marxist edifice in a new way. It only "produces a possible multiplicity of Marxisms," concludes Laruelle, "within *the* tradition."[12]

The fragmentation of the Marxist edifice is a problem for some philosophers and for others it is an instance of postmodern eclecticism to be celebrated and politically validated. For Laruelle, both perspectives are confused. Neither sees the unified theory that exists in and through the multiplicity of Marxisms. This is no less true of Marx's own texts and interventions. Consider that Marx produced philosophical, economic, polemical, and journalistic texts. Some philosophers will hunt for the red thread that links these. And others will celebrate the differences. Laruelle proposes another reading. Marx's work (and the Marxist tradition) is an instance of thought that is one and many. To reduce it to a singular ontology or else ontologize it as a plurality is "from our [non-Marxist] point of view ... entirely philosophical."[13] The quest to find or found the philosophy of Marx is rejected. Laruelle instead reads the pluralism of Marx's work as symptomatic of a singular refusal to reduce the Real to a single Philosophical Decision.

Non-Marxism takes as its point of departure the supposed "failure" of Marxism. The political "failures" of twentieth-century state socialism have led many thinkers to either abandon Marxist theory or to attempt to re-philosophize it in a way that appears more promising. Laruelle rejects both positions. Instead, he advocates for "taking Marxism out of the most philosophical premises and define it by its kernel which is irreducible, and foreign to philosophy?"[14] But this paradoxically requires doing philosophy, albeit in non-standard ways. This practice Laruelle traces back to Marx himself. "The wager hazarded here," writes Laruelle, "is this: the use of philosophy by Marxism ... is already a 'nonphilosophical' practice of philosophy, even if this practice is formulated ... with philosophical means."[15] The aim then is to render explicit and intensify Marx's non-philosophical logic in order to "philosophically impoverish Marxism through a voluntary pauperization."[16]

Non-Marxism aims to philosophically impoverish Marxism. *But this impoverishment works through philosophy in a non-standard way.* Here the concept of "introduction" is decisive. Laruelle's *Introduction to Non-Marxism* is (as its title plainly tells us) an "introduction" to non-Marxism. It is a rich conceptual resource. But it is clearly impoverished in one respect: it studiously avoids any claim to know or decide the Real, nor does it singularize the meaning of the Marxian corpus, nor finally does it essentialize it as a non-singular plurality. To impoverish Marxism means voiding its material of any epistemic pretensions concerning the Real. But that does *not* mean voiding it of theoretical and philosophical materials that serve the aim of liberating it from its standard philosophical limits and trappings. Non-Marxism is no more a vulgar anti-intellectualism than is non-philosophy in general. *To liberate Marxism from standard philosophy is a complex theoretical problem.*

Constellation as Method

The method I employ in this book is that of "constellation." A brief review of this concept is in order before turning to a brief overview of the chapters to follow. In *Negative Dialectics*, Theodor Adorno develops Walter Benjamin's concept of "constellation," which the latter first articulated in *The Origin of German Tragic Drama*. Benjamin there analogizes the relation of concepts to objects as that of stars to constellations. "Ideas are to objects as constellations are to stars."[17] Benjamin argues for a neo-Kantian distinction between idea and concept. Adorno transforms Benjamin's raw material into a non-Kantian thesis concerning the "disenchantment of the concept."[18] Adorno reformulates Benjamin's analogy: *constellations are to stars as concepts are to objects; they are radically distinct.* Objects of reality can never be adequately encompassed by concepts. "In fact no philosophy, not even extreme empiricism," writes Adorno, "can drag in the *facta bruta* and present them like cases in anatomy or experiments in physics."[19] Concepts like constellations are imposed on brute facts. Concepts and constellations are also historical through and through. The constellations of the night sky are projected patterns of human thought and human history. Adorno's "disenchantment" dictates that philosophy self-critically come to terms with its radical finitude. "Necessity compels philosophy to operate with concepts," writes Adorno, "but this necessity must not be turned into the virtue of their priority."[20] Adorno and Laruelle are affine here.

Adorno and Laruelle work with philosophical materials while underscoring the non-coincidence or "non-identity" (in Adornian language) between concept and Real. Theory thus becomes the art of diagramming the perpetual failure to establish an identity between concept and Real. "As a constellation, theoretical thought circles the concept it would like to unseal," writes Adorno, "hoping that it may fly open like the lock of a well-guarded safe-deposit box; in response not to a single key or a single number, but to a combination of numbers."[21] The only way to unseal the concept from its self-assured philosophical sufficiency is to circle it with a constellation or combination of concepts that unlock the "well-guarded" secret of the concept's epistemic insufficiency.

Likewise, Laruelle's method treats philosophy as raw materials for thinking in non-standard ways. Non-philosophical "operations determine a new conditioning or usage of philosophy."[22] Non-philosophy reconditions the material of philosophy by *treating it as raw material*. "Philosophy and science, art, ethics, etc.," writes Laruelle, "do not come into non-philosophy as such or as themselves, but as *provisions* ... simple provisions, which is to say in-the-last-instance simple phenomena."[23] Philosophy as such is not the content of non-philosophy. Rather, philosophy as raw materials—words, concepts, terms, theses—are themselves treated as material without any special claim or decisive bearing on the Real. Concepts *qua* material become what Laruelle elects to call "clones" of their former philosophical selves. There is an elective affinity here too with Adorno. Constellations (*pace* Adorno) are composed of self-critically "disenchanted" concepts; "clones" (*pace* Laruelle) are composed of provisional philosophical materials voided of their claims on the Real. In each case, the method serves to treat *concepts as concepts* without confusing or conflating them with the Real. My method draws on Adorno and Laruelle in an attempt to explicate, contextualize, and develop non-Marxism by situating it within a set of affine philosophical constellations.

This book is organized around five constellations: stranger, struggle, impossibilization, fiction, and metaphysics. Each term names a constellation that encircles a set of problems and themes in Laruelle's non-Marxist work. "Stranger" names procedures that estrange philosophical materials without depriving thought of its material resources. "Struggle" names the problem of the relation between theory and political practice and the immanent necessity to struggle against the merely *philosophical solutions* that have traditionally framed this problem. "Impossibilization" is an invented name for a process of thinking and writing that takes the supposed "failure" of Marxism as the point of departure only to radicalize its potential for the transformation of thought. "Fiction" names a mode of thinking and writing that fictionalizes the resources of Marxist theory in order to open a utopic perspective in non-dialectical terms. "Metaphysics" names the core of Katerina Kolozova's important and decisive development of non-Marxist theory, or what I call the "Kolozovan variant." These five constellations are arranged using a wide array of philosophical and theoretical raw material drawn from a variety of Marxist traditions. But I want to be clear: the names that appear in this book—Louis Althusser, Theodor Adorno, Jean Baudrillard, Katerina Kolozova, Karl Marx, as well as François Laruelle and others—are conceived *allegorically as figures of thought* who figure and animate my constellations. My aim is to demonstrate the potentiality of non-Marxism through these figures without reifying any one or number of them.

Politically, my reading of Laruelle's work is that it gives us raw materials with which to make a strike against the logical imperatives of exchange and equivalence that underwrite the constitution and circulation of values in the capitalist and philosophical spheres; to cancel the mechanisms of conceptual exchange whereby the Real is ideologically traded on the floating currency of philosophical and capitalist values. Let me be clear: *philosophy is not the enemy—it is the material.* The lesson of Laruelle's work is paradoxical that the only way to move beyond philosophy is to work through its materials. Non-philosophy's diagnosis of philosophy's disavowed insufficiency with respect to the Real reminds us that the Real is not philosophical: the Real is radical.

Outline of Chapters

Chapter 2 examines Marx's attempt to "estrange" philosophy. Drawing on the work of Georges Labica, Michel Henry, and others, I argue that the "early" Marx's attempt to distance his work from standard philosophy required a traversal through it in order to uncover resources for its surpassal. I argue that Marx's concept of estrangement provides the raw material for Laruelle's conception of the "individual," the "stranger," and, finally, for what can be rightly called a "stranger Marxism."

Chapter 3 examines the concept of struggle in non-Marxism in light of the question of theory and practice. I situate Laruelle's clone of struggle in light of the work of Louis Althusser and Mario Tronti. Althusser (even in his later works) emphasizes the necessity and autonomy of theory while Tronti stresses the need to formulate theory in light of the thought immanent to practical political struggle. The chapter turns on the question of what it means to struggle in theoretical practice and what this entails for Laruelle's theorization of the "non-proletarian," the "subject-in-struggle," and the "generically" human or "the victim."

Chapter 4 interrogates the structuralist dimension of non-philosophy. The argument proceeds via a reading of Laruelle's concept of Philosophical Decision as a quasi-structuralist judgment on the nature of philosophy. It then moves to a discussion of what I take to be a structurally affine relation between the negative dialectics of Adorno and Laruelle's argument concerning the epistemic insufficiency of philosophical concepts. The impossibility of the epistemic capture of the Real is refunctioned by Laruelle as a negative thesis on the radicality of the Real in the last instance.

Chapter 5 examines the status of theoretical writing in Laruelle. Laruelle's axiomatic insistence that concepts and the Real are not equivalent or exchangeable yields a fictionalization of Marxian theory.

The chapter examines this via a comparative reading of the "philo-fiction" of Laruelle and the "theory-fiction" of Jean Baudrillard. Both thinkers in different ways faced the problem of how to write theory in the face of the radical foreclosure of the Real (*pace* Laruelle) or the "death of the Real" (*pace* Baudrillard). Their work provides us with a wealth of resources for "fictionalizing" theory and representing it in a non-dialectical form that as such cancels the logic of exchange and equivalence.

Chapter 6 examines the non-Marxist work of Katerina Kolozova. Her reformulation of non-Marxism, which I call the "Kolozovan variant," is centered on the radicality of physicality and the necessity of metaphysics. Kolozova develops a radical theory of the human that challenges standard philosophies of humanism and its posthumanist and anti-humanist variants. The Kolozovan variant represents a key development within non-Marxist theory that importantly mobilizes it within contemporary developments in gender theory and post-anthropocentric theorizations while calling for a fundamental critique of philosophical "materialism."

Chapter 7 offers a review of the material covered and suggests what the political relevance of doing theory in the present crisis might be. My hope is that this book enables readers to engage Laruelle's work (perhaps for the first time) and to grasp the importance of situating and contextualizing non-Marxism without reducing it to standard philosophy.

2

Stranger

Perhaps it is a symptom of the age of philosophical Marxism that one enters its domain with trepidation. The bewildering number of competing theories, schools, and traditions make any foray into Marxist theory daunting. This chapter focuses on the concept of "estrangement" in the early Marx. I argue that this concept is cloned in Laruelle's work in order to establish a "stranger Marxism" radically estranged from the supercapitalist ideologies that haunt philosophical Marxism. This non-Marxist perspective is established in the name of what Laruelle, building on Michel Henry, identifies as the "ordinary" or "generic" individual who is irreducible to the abstractions of philosophy and capital.

Thought Control

"Despite what appears to many as philosophy's benign, abstracted appearance," notes John O'Maoilearca, it is "the supreme form of thought control, or, to be perfectly clear, a device for controlling what counts as thought."[1] The objective of philosophical practice *qua* Philosophical Decision "is to capture everything under its own authority," writes O'Maoilearca, "its definitions of reality, knowledge, and, most particularly, thinking itself—an aristocratism of thinking."[2] This aristocratism of philosophy cannot easily be toppled in part because it is so foundational to the very practice of thought as we know it. This may at first sound strange. Anyone who has taught at a university or college can see clearly that philosophy and the humanities as a whole are radically marginalized. But the professional discipline of philosophy is only the tip of the iceberg of philosophical thought as a whole. The standard philosophical form of thinking—a decisionist form of thinking—is pervasive and extends well beyond the campus grounds. O'Maoilearca writes:

> Despite appearances to the contrary, philosophy remains our dominant form of knowledge, according to Laruelle. Or rather, it is the very form of domination within knowledge. Adopting many shapes and poses (empiricism, rationalism, idealism, materialism, scientism, even anti-philosophy), its fundamental pose is as a form of exemplary thinking. It is the model for all foundational thinking, even when those foundations are differential and antifoundational.[3]

The pervasive decisionist impulse of philosophy operates wherever and whenever one spontaneously decides on what counts as rational, reasonable, idealistic, materialistic, religious, and so on. Such decisions are made in casual conversations, in legislative chambers, in discussions of economic policy, in classrooms, in job interviews, and so on. These decisions all in one way or another proclaim what thinking (or at least good thinking) is. Take, for example, the ease with which we use the phrase "he's just not thinking." When what one really means is that "I don't agree." Philosophy *qua* Philosophical Decision auto-legislates what counts as thought. Hence, one does not need to produce a philosophical theory to be a philosopher in Laruelle's terms. Philosophy, for Laruelle, is not a discrete discipline, but a way of thinking that takes as its task to decide the Real and likewise to decide what counts as genuine thinking. "Understood in this fashion, philosophy is also the authoritarian structure of thinking that can operate in numerous domains," writes O'Maoilearca, "whether or not *we* call them 'philosophy.' "[4]

Philosophy understands itself as self-sufficient. Its self-understanding is that it possesses all the necessary resources with which to render a judgment on what counts as thought and what is Real. O'Maoilearca writes:

> Such a self-promoting thought—is not tethered to certain names or historical disciplines: as Laruelle has said in a recent interview, "every discipline very soon arrives at its own sufficiency, in the sense that it tends to auto-finalize itself, raise itself to the level of a total, complete or all-powerful [thought]." ... Philosophy is a vector ... it is a "phase state" in thought rather than any universally acknowledged 'content,' one that gives itself sovereign power of thought over all others, whether they be philosophers or non-philosophers.[5]

I am reminded of what William James once noted in his lectures on pragmatism: "Philosophy is at once the most sublime and most trivial of human pursuits."[6] It produces great and weighty books, but it is also the most trivial of gestures as Laruelle and O'Maoilearca point out. For James, philosophy is a state of mind, a "temperament," or, in Laruelle's terms, a "posture" in thought. One might, for example, adopt the posture of the materialist at the bank; or that of the idealist in politics; or that of the religiously minded in moments of existential dread. And one might do all this in a single day.

Philosophies are something we inhabit in different ways at different times. James readily concedes that no philosopher is likely to admit this, because it would have the effect of reducing the grandeur of philosophy to contrasting and contingently inhabited moods or postures or states of mind. But if one does admit to it, as James and Laruelle do in different ways, then one can begin to see the whole of philosophy very differently than how it is presented in many university classrooms. I myself have come to see philosophy through non-philosophy as something more like an artisanal craft or perhaps even a form of art. But at the very least I see it as a creative practice. As Anthony Paul Smith notes:

> Fundamental to Laruelle's understanding of thought is that it is a human activity, a human practice. When human (beings) engage in theory, they are in the midst of creating something, they are in the midst of labor, and are fashioning something from the material around them. It is in many ways beautiful, and anyone may know that beauty if they have ever fallen in love with an idea, or derived pleasure from reading a book or from writing an essay.[7]

The non-philosophical posture takes philosophy as a *physical process*. We fall in love or fall out of love with the materiality of philosophical words. The process of writing or reading theory is a pleasure (or at times an agony). It is felt in the body. The idea *qua* immaterial ensconced in a Platonic heaven has no credence in non-philosophy. Philosophy has traditionally relied on metaphors of distance especially "critical distance" above all else. It doesn't want to get too close. The philosopher's mind must always be kept at a respectable distance from the body. Non-philosophy proposes to do exactly the opposite by treating concepts as "physical" and immanent to the Real in the last instance. As O'Maoilearca explains:

> So what is unusual, and undoubtedly counterintuitive, about non-philosophy is the consistency with which it materializes all thought, including its own, within a radically *immanent* approach: it renders transcendence as immanence, as "position." This immanentist stance thereby sees philosophical thinking as both a performance *and* a physical tendency or spatial *activity*.[8]

Non-philosophy (in all its forms, including non-Marxism) is committed to the radical thesis that philosophy not only has a material basis, but that it is itself a material and physical practice. This is an empirical point: philosophy is made by thinking bodies manipulating or shaping, words, phrases, and sentences. And that is why (in part) non-Marxism draws considerable sustenance from the "early Marx" (particularly as articulated in Kolozova's work). The early Marx (before *Capital*) mounted a series of arguments against philosophical abstractionism and estrangement in the name of the physical and sensual. It is to this concept of estrangement in Marx and to the "stranger" in Laruelle that I now turn in an effort to elucidate a "stranger Marxism" than we have known.

Stranger

Marx was somewhat a stranger in the fields in which he worked. He rejected many of their cherished assumptions. Marx drew on recent German philosophy, but he rejected the assumptions of idealism. He drew upon classical political economy, but he rejected classical assumptions about the fairness of the market. As Laruelle notes:

> Marx used philosophy without being (entirely and spontaneously) a philosopher. He used science without being (entirely and spontaneously) a scientist. Neither idealism nor positivism, but two paths that form only one: not dialectically or according to other synthesis of deviations so as to form a kind of orthodoxy, but in an immanent manner through an identity of which we will say that it is *cloned* by the Real.[9]

We should pause to note the parenthetical phrase "entirely and spontaneously" as it is key to Laruelle's point. Marx was not "entirely or spontaneously" a philosopher or a scientist; indeed, he remained critically estranged from the then dominant worldviews circumscribed by each discipline, namely, positivistic science and idealist philosophy. To remain critically estranged in a state of self-imposed disciplinary exile was an ethical task. Only from this point of self-imposed exile could Marx enter the terrains of philosophy and science without simplistically subordinating his thought to their authority. Marx worked within philosophy and science while submitting to what Kolozova calls "the *diktat* of the real."[10] Marx critiqued philosophy and modern science ultimately for their failure to capture the complexities of reality. In this sense, his work was conditioned or "cloned" by the

Real to put the matter in non-philosophical terms. Here it will be useful to better situate Laruelle's method of "cloning" which estranges and makes the art of thinking stranger than standard philosophy. "The clone is expressed or articulates itself via non-philosophy," writes Laruelle, "not via philosophy as a material for cloning, even less from the Real which, without being transformed, is made a transcendental agent or essence of the Stranger-subject."[11] A difficult sentence to be sure. But not unintelligible. "Clone" is the name of philosophical material transformed in light of the axiom of the foreclosure of the Real. Philosophical material axiomatically voided of the power to decide the Real is "transcendental" insofar as it transcends the limits of philosophical decisionism: it transcends the decisional posture of standard philosophy. Cloned material *looks like* philosophy, but it is critically estranged from the Real. *But precisely in that estrangement it negatively mimics or clones the Real's indifference to thought.* One of the reasons why Laruelle's prose can be so tortured is that he attempts to write against the pull of Philosophical Decision and this requires relentless scrutiny of rhetoric and syntax in order to theoretically ensure that the prose of non-philosophy remains estranged from the lures and traps of Philosophical Decision and faithful to the radicality of the Real. The ethical imperative to estrange concepts from a decisionist dynamic is one of the chief ways that Laruelle clones Marx's concept of estrangement into the syntax of non-Marxism.

Estrangement

Marx's concept of estrangement, articulated first in *1844 Manuscripts*, has generated much debate and contestation. Althusser—whose work has been decisive for Laruelle's—famously rejected the concept of estrangement as "ideological" on the grounds that it is derived from a conception of "man's essence" that formed the keystone of modern bourgeois philosophy. But Althusser's sweeping indictment of the early Marx appears far more equivocal in the one essay he devotes to *1844 Manuscripts*. Allow me to quote Althusser at length on this point:

> One day we shall have to study this text [*1844 Manuscripts*] in detail and give a word-by-word explanation of it; discuss the theoretical status and theoretical role assigned to they key concept of alienated [or estranged] labor; examine this notion's conceptual field; and recognize that it does fill the role Marx then assigned it, the role of original basis [for a critique of political economy] but also that it can only fill this role so long as it *receives it* as a mandate and commission from a whole *conception of Man* which can derive from the *essence of Man* … In short, we shall have to discover beneath these terms … a future meaning, the meaning that still keeps them prisoners of a philosophy that is exercising its last prestige and power over them.[12]

The above passage is symptomatically marked by Althusser's "anti-humanist" reading of Marx. What is signified in these words is his anti-humanist critique of the concept of the "essence of Man" that for Althusser (and many of his generation) will come to define their historical and theoretical moment. "Man" formed the "original basis," argues Althusser, for Marx's nascent critique of political economy. But at this stage, according to Althusser, Marx's thought was still a prisoner to bourgeois humanism. The *1844 Manuscripts* mounts its critique of capital on an ethical commitment to the foundational concept of the "essence of Man" as a being endowed with inherent dignity. Marx in 1844, argues Althusser, was still too much of a bourgeois humanist to recognize that his discovery of political economy had in fact destroyed the "original basis" for his humanist critique of capital. A powerful thesis. But why did Althusser postpone the act of reading *1844 Manuscripts* without postponing judgment on this text? Is this symptomatic of Althusser's rush to secure Marx's name for the anti-humanist cause? Perhaps now is the time to read. I will focus on just two passages from *1844 Manuscripts* where the thematic of estrangement presents itself most acutely at the economic and philosophic levels. Marx writes:

> The *devaluation* of the world of men is in direct proportion to the *increasing value* of the world of things. Labor produces not only commodities: it produces itself and the worker as a *commodity* – and this at the same rate as that which it produces commodities in general. This fact expresses merely that the object which labor produces – labor's product – confronts it as something alien, as a power independent of the producer. The product of labor is labor which has been embodied in an object, which has become material: it is the *objectification* of labor ... Under these economic conditions this realization of labor appears a *loss of realization* for the workers; objectification as *loss of the object and bondage to it*; appropriation as *estrangement*.[13]

The "devaluation" of men or persons is in direct proportion to the "increasing value" of things. What are things of value in 1844?

Answer: commodities. The increasing commodification of work is in direct proportion to the devaluation of people's time and labor. Increased production increases the number of workers and further fragments the production process decreasing the "value" of each unit of commodified labor. Value is drained from the worker's work and is "realized" in the value of the commodities produced. But the value of work and workers is "derealized" in direct proportion to the realization of commodity value achieved on the market. Workers are thereby held in bondage to the decreasing value of their work and increasingly "estranged" from the value realized by commodities on the market. Marx writes that this "estrangement is manifested not only in the result, but in the *act of production*, within the *producing activity*, itself. How could the worker come to face the product of his activity as a stranger, were it not that in the very act of production he was estranging himself from himself?"[14] It is the very act of producing commodities that produces the worker as a stranger to himself. What emerges in the act of commodity production is a self that is stranger to the self *qua* worker. The estranged self–repelled, expelled, exiled— produced out of the reflux of commodified labor negatively indexes a subjectivity which cannot be easily assimilated into the rigors and discipline of work. And we know this too well. We feel it not only in the exhaustion from work, but in the exhaustion *with work* itself.

As noted, Althusser and his students pilloried the "early" Marx's "ideological" reliance on an "essentialist" concept of the human. But others in the 1960s took a different view. Michel Henry, for one, argues that Althusser fails to understand that Marx (including the early Marx) did embark on a critique of the "essence of man," but in so doing he salvaged a new concept of the "individual." Henry writes:

Marx has indeed abandoned this concept [of the essence of man], not after his earlier writings but in these very early writings. The entire fundamental philosophical problem of the early Marx is precisely this rejection of the essence of man, the essence of the species ... However, Marx's problematic rejecting of the philosophy of the essence of man does not entail a dismissal of the individual *qua* real individual.[15]

A new concept of the "individual," according to Henry, grounds Marx's consistent critique of essentialist concepts of the human. Marx, according to Henry, shows that any attempt to ground the human on concepts derived from biology, psychology, or sociology fails to capture in its concepts what radically resists every such philosophical generalization; what Henry describes as "the most radical and most particular determination–the individual."[16] Marx's new conception of the individual, according to Henry, sets his work apart from that of the Young Hegelians. Their concept of estrangement, notes Henry, "consists of a representation, an act of thinking. But the whole problem of the early Marx consists precisely in exceeding this ideological concept of alienation [or estrangement] and rejecting it."[17] Marx understood that estrangement is not just a matter of how one thinks or represents oneself to oneself. If that were all estrangement is then "it suffices to represent things differently," notes Henry, "to stop representing one's essence outside one's self. It suffices to think differently."[18] This is what Marx rejects. Henry writes:

> Marx responds [to the Young Hegelians], in effect: you might very well represent things differently for yourself and change your concepts, but this has no importance. Thought cannot do anything

against reality, namely, the living individual in the first place, with its existing determinations, because this real, living, determined individual is completely different from the way in which he represents things and the way he represents himself, his "consciousness."[19]

Laruelle affirms Henry's central and radical thesis: *thought cannot do anything against reality*. The alienation or estrangement experienced by an individual is not a matter of thinking. Contra our postmodern managerial elite, the problem is not with one's attitude toward work. The problem is the reality of work itself. Henry (following Marx) conceives the individual not as the philosophical subject *par excellence*, but the name for what cannot be captured by any philosophic or economic system or abstract generalization.

Laruelle clones Henry's insight into what he terms the "finite individual." The concept of the "finite individual" is explored in greater depth in the next chapter. But suffice to say here that by "finite individual," Laruelle means that the most "ordinary" or "generic" reality of being human cannot be fully captured or assimilated by any philosophical theory of humanism, anti-humanism, or posthumanism. These "isms" are "infinite" schemes of the philosophical imagination. The human can be endlessly philosophized. But the real human—the human *in* the Real—is not a philosophical concept. Hence, for Laruelle a science of the human—as against the human sciences or humanities—should take as its point of departure the negative kernel at the heart of infinitized schemes of speculation on the human. The science of the human is a radical description of the lived experience of humanness or what Laruelle calls a "biography of ordinary man." Laruelle writes:

This is the meaning of "biography of ordinary man": a rigorous description of the most general experiences that govern the relation of individuals as such to History, to the State, to Economy, to Language, etc. The text of this science is thus no longer the *cogito* and its *membra disjecta*, which the Human Sciences divide among themselves. It is this irreducible kernel that must be extracted from the cogito in which it is still enclosed and concealed.[20]

The "ordinary" human is never captured entirely by the philosophical schemes of History, State, Economy, or Language. These are proper names for philosophies that envision human beings as "products of their time" (History), citizens and non-citizens (State), workers and owners (Economy), grammatical subjects (Language), and so on. These according to Laruelle are just different versions of the philosophy of the *cogito* and its deconstructed remainders. None of these captures the "real" human—that radically recalcitrant "kernel"—which cannot be reduced to an abstraction. The thinking, willing, intentional, "subject"—the "cogito" and its variations—misses what is finite, but also that which negatively transcends the infinitizing logic of philosophical speculation. The lived experience in being human—that which is "given"—and cannot be reduced to thought is where a non-philosophical science of human description must begin.

Laruelle draws on Marx's concept of estrangement but he radicalizes it. For Laruelle, one is not a worker, a citizen, an economic unit of value, nor, finally, a philosophical "subject," not even the subject of Marxist philosophy or revolutionary praxis. The finite individual is stranger to all of these and stranger than all these. In non-philosophy, the "Self and the Stranger stop being opposed," writes Laruelle, "stop being face to face and at war. They are identical-in-the-last-instance."[21] The estrangement between, for example, worker and individual is not, for Laruelle, resolvable according to any dialectic. The worker's estrangement reveals only that she is simultaneously stranger and subject or "Stranger-subject" as Laruelle terms it.

We are, for Laruelle, strangers to supercapitalist abstractions in the last instance and thus permanently estranged and exiled from the familiar terrains encompassed by philosophies of the subject and the human. The problem then for non-Marxism is to render Marxism strange or estranged from philosophy. How is this to be accomplished? What does it mean to practice Marxism strangely? Here we must return to Marx.

Marx's Sojourn in Philosophy

Marx traversed through philosophy to expose its ideological basis. In *The German Ideology*, for example, Marx and Engels critique the ideology of "German criticism" from Kant to the Young Hegelians. "German criticism has, right up to its latest efforts," writes Marx and Engels, "never quitted the realm of philosophy."[22] Marx repudiated the idealist tradition for spiriting away historical reality. Marx did, however, give passing marks to Feuerbach for his historicization of religious doctrine. But the efforts of this Young Hegelian (as with the rest) did not go far enough for Marx.

The only results which this philosophic criticism could achieve were a few (and at that thoroughly one-sided) elucidations of Christianity from the point of view of religious history; all the rest of their assertions are only further embellishments of their claim to have furnished, in these unimportant elucidations, discoveries of universal importance. It has not occurred to any one of these philosophers to inquire into the connection of German philosophy with German reality, the relation of their criticism to their own material surroundings.[23]

Feuerbach (and the Young Hegelians as a whole) were right to insist that religious propositions were matters of history and not of transhistorical revelation. But he did not see that *this is true of philosophy too*.

But Marx's most biting attack on Feuerbach was aimed at the latter's "materialism." In *Theses on Feuerbach*, Marx indicts *philosophical materialism* (and all philosophy). Marx asserts there that all philosophy—even so-called "materialism"—is speculative in the last instance. The "chief defect" of all philosophy is that "the object, reality, what we apprehend through our senses, is understood only in the form of the *object of contemplation*; but not as *sensuous human activity*."[24] What *philosophical materialism* conceptualizes as reality is only ever an "object of contemplation." It cannot grasp sensuous human activity, because while this can be converted into concepts, it is what Adorno rightly calls *nonconceptual* in the last instance.

Marx's blunt refusal of philosophy in the last instance and the gesture toward a non-philosophical (in Marx's sense) outside makes philosophers uncomfortable. Étienne Balibar, for one, argues that Marx's repudiation of philosophy is equivocal at best. Balibar writes:

> *Theses on Feuerbach* … demand a definitive exit (*Ausgang*) from philosophy … [but the] difficulties begin at precisely this point. There can be no doubt that Marx never ventured to publish a call for such an exit or did not find an opportunity to do so. And yet he wrote it and, like a "purloined letter," it has come down to us.[25]

Balibar arguably places undue emphasis on the fact that Marx did not publish *Theses on Feuerbach* in his lifetime as proof that he was equivocal about calling for an exit from philosophy. But, as Balibar notes, Marx wrote it and "it has come down to us" with all the difficulties it presents for Marxist philosophy. Balibar's solution is that we should interpret *Theses on Feuerbach* as a polemic against philosophical speculation enunciated from inside speculative philosophy. The call for an exit from philosophy is "ensconced not just at the heart of philosophy," writes Balibar, "but at the heart of its most speculative turn, in which it strives to *think its own limits*, whether to abolish them or to establish itself on the basis of a recognition of those limits."[26] Marx's "purloined letter" is to be read, on Balibar's reading, as a speculation on the limits of speculation, but not a "published" call to exit philosophy. The form of *Theses on Feuerbach* is some evidence for Balibar's reading. Not an argument nor simply a polemic, but a series of seemingly speculative and provisional points of departure for a thinking that identifies the ideological limits of speculation. Balibar's reading is impressive and concise. But I believe that no one has thought to the limit the question of the equivocal status of philosophy for Marx more assiduously than Georges Labica. It is to his work that I now turn for a moment.

Firstly, Labica argues that Marx's "sojourn in philosophy" must be understood in the social context of the dominance of "German criticism." Marx could not simply exit philosophy in the first (or perhaps even the last) instance because historically speaking he was forced to think through philosophy as philosophy was the horizon in which social and political questions were posed at that time. To understand Marx, it is necessary to understand "the necessity of the sojourn in philosophy," writes Labica, "a necessity which in fact was uniquely imperative in Germany; which was, in fact, a property of the German situation, in which philosophy (or, in more general terms, theoretical reflection) seemed to constitute the sole available medium for social criticism."[27]

Marx's work, especially *The German Ideology*, *Theses on Feuerbach*, and *The Poverty of Philosophy*, are testaments to the necessity of his "sojourn in philosophy." The ideology that is challenged in these texts is precisely the ideological assumption that philosophy is sufficient to accomplish a meaningful critique of ideology in the first place. Hence, in these texts, the struggle by the Young Hegelians to reconcile thought and the historical world is affirmed by Marx but *not* their solution. Labica writes:

> it was the merit of Marx to recognize and to show that behind this alternative, implicit in the suggested relation philosophy/the world, was hidden another alternative, which invoked the first and held it up to comparison in order to lay bare the conditions of its possibility and to ask it precisely the question of its questions: was

this relation, however conceived, to remain forever internal to philosophy, or did its very presence reveal an outer world which, unbeknown to philosophy, was philosophy's presupposition?[28]

Labica's insight here is profound. The question that Marx put to philosophy is the "question of its questions." Is the relation between philosophy and the world a question that has to be asked forever and always within philosophy? Or, and this is Labica's position, does the very presence of the problem within philosophy presuppose something non-philosophical in the last instance? Marx's "sojourn in philosophy" was motivated by a search for the starting-point for the question or the problem of the relation of philosophy to the world. Labica's thesis rings with a decidedly proto-Laruellean tone.

> The "real": this was the starting-point of Marx's quest. But this real had nothing to do with any empirical given, it was not to be arrived at by placing, in opposition to juridical ideas, the forms of existence to which they [philosophical ideas] were inadequate. It designated the inner emptiness of the ideas themselves and the arbitrary character of the systems into which they could be organized.[29]

Marx's "sojourn in philosophy," according to Labica, was historically necessary because philosophy was paradoxically where Marx's generation felt it had to begin to search for the real that negatively indexed itself within philosophy. Marx, however, distanced his work from that of the Young Hegelians by rejecting the "juridical" (read "epistemological") problematic of how to judge the relation between philosophical speculation and the Real. He took as given that the Real could not be captured adequately by philosophy and therefore suspended the problem posed by that question. Marx's "sojourn in philosophy" aimed at exposing the ideology of German philosophy and philosophy as such.

Theses on Feuerbach, *The German Ideology*, and *The Poverty of Philosophy* stand as instances not only where philosophy is thinking its limits (*pace* Balibar), but instances where the question of the relation of thought and the Real is suspended from within philosophy in order to expose the historical conditions for philosophical reason that (like religion in the past) for a time constituted the horizon in which the problem of the real (*pace* Labica) or the Real (*pace* Laruelle) seemingly had to be posed. Labica rejects the popular claim that the "mature" Marx of *Capital* either simply abandoned philosophy or did not spell it out. Labica advises that we take seriously the subtitle of *Capital*: "a *critique* of political economy." *Capital* is a critique of the reigning philosophy of Marx's day that—though it was disavowed by "empirical" economists—underwrote their assumptions about the nature of the individual, society, and rationality. The ground for Marx's critique of philosophy in *Capital* was presaged already in his critique of the thought of Pierre-Joseph Proudhon in *The Poverty of Philosophy* (a mocking play on Proudhon's *The Philosophy of Poverty*) to which we now turn.

We should first note that Marx's critique of Proudhon is a critique of his *philosophy*. Marx was otherwise supportive of Proudhon's work. He was particularly appreciative of Proudhon's effort to theorize political economy from the perspective of working-class interests. But he rejects Proudhon's insistence that the estrangement by labor can be resolved from within the limits of capital. Proudhon fails to accomplish a sufficiently self-critical evaluation of the philosophical assumptions that underwrite his economic recommendations and of the economic realities that he abstracts away in his more philosophical moments. Proudhon's tendency to abstractly address lived realities is seen by Marx as a symptom of the disease of philosophy as a whole. Marx's 1847 foreword puts the matter succinctly.

> M. Proudhon has the misfortune of being peculiarly misunderstood in Europe. In France, he has the right to be a bad economist, because he is reputed to be a good German philosopher. In Germany, he has the right to be a bad philosopher, because he is reputed to be one of the ablest French economists. Being both German and economist at the same time, we desire to protest against this double error. The reader will understand that in this thankless task we have often had to abandon our criticism of M. Proudhon in order to criticize German philosophy, and at the same time to give observations on political economy.[30]

Proudhon must be attacked *philosophically* not because philosophy needs to be saved from the hands of an inept practitioner. Rather, he must be attacked philosophically in order to expose how Proudhon's philosophy distorts his economic recommendations. The attack on Proudhon (not unlike that on Feuerbach) exposes the emptiness of philosophical ideas in order to critically confront and theoretically counter the reality of lived suffering under the economic and philosophical order of capitalism. Marx shows that "Proudhon gestures in the direction of Feuerbach," notes Labica, "and raises the question of the status of philosophy"[31] Marx's philosophical attacks on Proudhon and Feuerbach expose the ideological distortions that *philosophizing* social conditions creates. According to Labica,

Marx's critiques of Feuerbach and Proudhon index a possible exit from philosophy by passing through philosophy in a novel way. On this score, Labica and Henry could not be further apart in their interpretation of Marx's relation to philosophy.

Henry sides with Balibar's view, namely, that the exit (*Ausgang*) from philosophy is a fundamental misreading of Marx's work. Henry argues that Marx used philosophy principally to clarify and critique the philosophy of bourgeois economic science. Henry writes:

> [T]he analysis that comes to destroy this appearance, that solves the enigma, that clears away this mystification, is no longer an economic analysis, it is philosophy. It is clear then how wrong it is to present the evolution of Marx's thought as the progressive or brutal abandonment of philosophy after his early writings, then reduced to a simple ideology, and this to the profit of a positive and purely scientific study of the economy.[32]

Marx, Henry argues, consistently demonstrates the *necessity of philosophy* to clear up the mystifications of economics. Marx's work—from the early to the late writings—is an argument for a *philosophy of economics*. On this reading, Marx's work resisted the pull of nineteenth-century positivist science. The dispute between Labica and Henry may be posed as the following question: does philosophy underwrite the *critical* dimension of Marx's work? Or is it something else? Althusser, for one, spent his career trying to discover the philosophy of the late Marx.

Althusser holds that Marx's oeuvre divides into three major periods: Early Works, Works of the Break, and the Mature Works. The thought of the early Marx (e.g., *1844 Manuscripts*) critiques capital from a "humanist" standpoint derived from the revolutionary philosophy of the bourgeois Enlightenment; the Marx of the "break" (e.g., *The German Ideology*) exposes the limits of humanist philosophy; and, finally the mature Marx (e.g., *Capital*) breaks decisively with humanism by articulating a fundamentally anti-humanist perspective. The question that Althusser asked was: what new philosophy underwrote this anti-humanism? Marx indicated the outlines of "dialectical materialism" in *Capital*, but it lay unfinished. Only a complete *philosophical account* of dialectical materialism, Althusser argued, could ensure the scientificity of Marx's historical materialism. "The novelty of dialectical materialism," notes Gregory Elliott in his study of Althusser, "was that with its arrival philosophy had passed 'from the condition of an *ideology* [to] a *scientific discipline*' – one capable of rendering a scientific account of its object: the history of the production of knowledge."[33] Althusser's work is explored in more depth in the next chapter, but I think it suffices here to note the gap between Henry's and Althusser's positions. Whereas Henry argues that Marx invented a new philosophy of the individual with which to combat the mystifications of economics, Althusser argues that Marx abandoned the humanist philosophy of his youth and founded the science of historical materialism, but left unfinished the philosophy of dialectical materialism that would have grounded it. The Marxism of the 1960s produced three entirely different readings of Marx's relation to philosophy: Marx exposed the ideology of philosophy (Labica), Marx used philosophy to expose the ideology of economics (Henry), Marx invented a new philosophy, but never completed it (Althusser). Laruelle draws on each of these readings to go beyond the dialectics of philosophical reading.

A Stranger Marxism

Laruelle is less concerned with adjudicating the question of which philosophies are present where and when in Marx's trajectory than in extending his combat against the reign of philosophical abstraction. It is the primacy of the Real that governs Laruelle's approach to the Marxist tradition. Every effort is made by Laruelle to resist the lure of deciding philosophically on Marx in the name of collating raw materials to develop his resistance to abstraction. This takes the form of a radically immanent way of thinking and writing that seeks to formally resist the decisionist dialectic by which the Real enters into a conceptual economy of exchange with philosophy. He formally renounces all conceptual hierarchies and insists on a "democracy of thought." This is not relativism. Rather, it is a perspective that is theoretically committed to the immanent thesis that all thought is insufficient to capture the Real, which is decisive in the last instance. In that minimal but critical sense "all thoughts are equal" to borrow the title of O'Maoilearca's pathbreaking study on Laruelle.[34]

Non-Marxism (and non-philosophy generally) is oriented toward the Real that it self-critically knows it cannot think. The non-conceptuality of the Real is cloned in non-philosophy as "force-(of)-thought"—a force on thought by what cannot be thought, the Real—but which Laruelle metaphorically envisions as "vision-in-One." "Vision-in-One" and "force-(of)-thought" function as operators in the writing of non-philosophical theoretical work. From the perspective of "vision-in-One," philosophies appear as materials epistemically equal only inasmuch as all philosophies equally fail to capture the Real. This perspective constitutes what Laruelle calls a "democracy of thought." "Here democracy is not an object of thought or reflection," writes Laruelle, "but the essence of knowledges produced by force (of) thought or in-the-last-instance by vision-in-One which protects … against any spirit of hierarchy."[35] From a non-philosophically de-hierarchized and defetishized perspective, philosophy appears as raw material. The problem that presents itself from this viewpoint is no longer a matter of deciding which philosophies are right. But rather the problem is: what can be done with these materials? The answer to that question in non-philosophy takes the form of a material practice that as a practice offers an immanent training in how to think philosophically without subordinating the Real to the logic of exchange and equivalence that underwrites the supercapitalist economy of knowledge production. Another question also appears from this vantage: what forms of writing and thinking need to be fashioned in order to do philosophy non-philosophically? The issue of form in non-philosophical thought and writing is examined in Chapter 5. But here I want to gloss the problem of form and to consider what this entails for the practice of non-Marxism.

Laruelle often employs the term "matrix" to denote the framework of non-philosophy. The non-philosophical matrix is established on the basis of its two principal axioms: the foreclosure of the Real to philosophy and correspondingly the insufficiency of standard philosophy with respect to the Real. Beyond this axiomatic standpoint, much of non-philosophy can be described not as a doctrine, but a doing. "The matrix of non-philosophy," writes Laruelle, "is a *speaking/thinking-according-to-the-One*."[36] To speak/think according to the One is to syntactically, rhetorically as well as conceptually compose in such a way that concepts are presented as physical materials immanent to the Real. Much of this cannot be done in any other way than by highly stylized and formal means that can make reading Laruelle difficult. But non-philosophy does not mean a rejection of philosophical materials: it means only a rejection of conceptual decisionism. One can only think *according to* the Real by thinking according to the "force" of its foreclosure to thought. There is no direct conceptual relation to the Real not even a non-philosophical relation. "There is no non-philosophical relation. To practice philosophy," writes Laruelle, "is to think by philosophical means, or other means that are *de jure* philosophizable, and in the end determined according-to-the Real."[37] Hence to think/do non-Marxism is *de jure* to think what is philosophizable in Marxism without thinking that in standard philosophical terms.

It must be noted that it would be quite easy here to assemble a thesis on Laruelle that attempts to situate his work within a preexistent philosophical conjuncture. Laruelle himself admits that, for example, one might situate the whole non-Marxist project within a field marked at its borders by the work of Spinoza and Henry. "For various doctrinal Marxists," writes Laruelle, "non-Marxism can seem very much on the surface, like a synthesis of Spinoza and Michel Henry."[38] It can seem this way because Laruelle affirms the immanent perspective of Spinoza and Henry as well as aspects of Henry's phenomenology, particularly in his emphasis on lived experience. But to reduce non-Marxism to that risks missing what is radically different about it. It would miss the way in which non-philosophical cloning fashions a different thought or, again, what Laruelle calls a "Stranger-subject." It is to this clone that I now turn to examine its implications for the concept of the individual, the proletariat, and for the practice of non-Marxism itself.

Stranger-subject

The "Stranger-subject" is the cloned form of the estranged subject in Marx's formulation of estrangement. "Stranger-subject" names the permanent estrangement of the ordinary or finite individual from philosophical or economic capture. But it also names "force-(of)-thought' as [the] real content of the 'proletariat.' "[39] The "real content of the proletariat" is a stranger subject than what we find in the pages of Marxist polemics. It is the concept of the proletariat voided of the decisionist frameworks of Marxist and bourgeois political thought. The "non-proletariat" is not a class, a person, or a political party. The "real content of the proletariat" or the "non-proletariat" is precisely this non-exchangeability and non-equivalence between the Real of lived immanence and the rationalized edifices of Marxist and bourgeois thought. The non-proletariat insists immanently as the symptomatic sign of the conceptual failures to capture and name it. Laruelle writes of the non-proletariat:

> It is only an immanent adversary *for* the capital-world, but … not immanent *to* the capital-world. It presents itself as the proto-originary, the first, adversary of the World, it is even the emergence of struggle and struggle *as such*. The non-proletarian subject is Other than the proletariat and is therefore not marked or chosen by capital, but fashioned by it.[40]

The non-proletariat is the cloned name for what cannot be reduced either to bourgeois philosophies of the subject nor class philosophies of Marxism nor any philosophical schema. It names what is excluded from the grid of philosophical intelligibility that Marxism and bourgeois thought impose upon people. The non-proletarian *qua* cloned concept is "fashioned" by capital, but it is not "marked" or "chosen" by the philosophies that have been fashioned by capital, namely Marxism and bourgeois political economy.

Non-Marxism is a radicalization of the critical project inaugurated by Marx. But, instead of a "critique of political economy," it aims to *produce a critique of the economy of philosophical production*, which rests on capitalist principles of exchange and equivalence whereby concepts are judged by their "purchase" on the Real. Any Marxism that trades in this conceptual economy reproduces the logic of exchange and equivalence that governs life under capital and thus *in theory* reproduces the logic of domination. "Non-Marxism is only a critique of Marxism that is at once immanent and heteronomous," writes Laruelle, "but it is first of all an explanatory theory, for explanation is the best critique of illusion, indeed of hallucination."[41] Non-Marxism works on Marxist materials in order to perform an immanent critique of the standard economy of philosophical production at the level of thought and that of economy in the name of all that has been excluded by Marxist and bourgeois political economy—the "non-proletariat." Non-Marxism consistently performs (not merely demonstrates) the insufficiency of economy and philosophy to the Real. "At bottom it is a matter of dismantling the *Principle of Sufficient Marxism*," writes Laruelle, "through a non-sufficient conception of the real base and infrastructure, which ... is an ontological non-sufficiency."[42] Non-Marxism does not attempt to provide that ontology or to contest it. It rather reduces the entire Marxist edifice to conceptual materials that can be reorganized in order to critique the illusion of Marxism's sufficiency and the sufficiency of philosophy generally.

To work in the non-Marxist register requires critical decisions both about how to approach Marxism and how to rewrite its philosophical syntax. "The non-Marxist decision," notes Laruelle, "is a transformation of the thought-world" of Marxist philosophy into a thought according to "the Stranger-subject."[43] This transformation of the thought-world of Marxism "excludes the idea of an inter-vention within the World."[44] It excludes any sense of "inter-vention" in that it excludes any philosophically oriented *venture* into the "World" understood by Laruelle as the hallucinated name for the Real constantly invoked by philosophers. Non-Marxism *does not intervene in the World of philosophy; it intervenes in the philosophical World.* "Marxism has necessarily confused," notes Laruelle, "the practical intervention into the World itself with the constitution and emergence of another city, a City of the Proletariat."[45] The object of non-Marxism is precisely the self-critical illumination of this non-coincidence between the City of Philosophy and lived life. This immanent critique of philosophy is undertaken by non-Marxism "without any possible reciprocation" between thought and the Real.[46] Non-Marxism is a relentlessly inward-turning critique that parasitically thrives on what it repudiates in order to model a thought faithful to the radicality of the Real.

Exit to Aesthetics

To conclude, I want to turn back to the question of an exit from philosophy by posing the possibility that the exit from philosophy after Laruelle might be best described as an exit for the entry door to aesthetics. This exit might seem more like a revolving door since we are used to thinking of aesthetics as a philosophical discipline. But the aesthetics I have in mind is modeled on Laruelle's conceptual work on photography.

In *The Concept of Non-Photography*, Laruelle inverts the reader's expectation for a new theory of photography. Instead what he offers is a critique of the photographic logic internal to the history of standard philosophy. Philosophy, argues Laruelle, has historically been consumed with not only the metaphoricity of light *qua* the "light of reason," but specifically with the aim to capture an image of the Real given as the concept World. This desire (sometimes disavowed and repressed) traverses philosophical history. Laruelle writes:

> No point in trying to separate philosophy from this photographic legend that encircles it: philosophy is nothing other than that legend of the fulgurant illumination of things ... that founds the photographocentric destiny of the West. Well before the invention of the corresponding technology, a veritable automatism of photographic repetition traverses western thought.[47]

The myth of the photographic-like capture of the Real in a philosophical image of the World is Laruelle's target here. The photographocentric bias is especially acute in standard philosophies of photography, which attempt to capture the Real of photography usually by taking some aspect—the camera, the subject, the photographer—as the essence of photography.

Laruelle proposes instead a theory of "non-photography" resistant to the decisionist impulse of standard philosophy. He opts to constitute "at least in principle" an "abstract theory of photography—but radically abstract, absolutely non-worldly and non-perceptual."[48] This theory in principle takes as its model what Laruelle calls "being-photo of the photo." This is not the photo considered (critically or not) as double of reality or even its photographic sign. The "being-photo of the photo" is that "nuance that separates the identity of photography ... from its being or its ontological interpretation."[49] Laruelle theoretically distinguishes photography *qua* photo from the *philosophical problem* of photography in order to work with the "[t]ruth-in-photo ... detained in the photograph itself."[50] Laruelle constructs a model for what non-philosophy—not only non-photography—can be, namely, a means of thinking the immanent truth of *conceptual materials as mere raw materials* and not reflections or "photographs" of the face of the Real.

The whole of *The Concept of Non-Photography* is a model for what doing non-philosophy looks like. It is a process of writing that is decidedly "non-figurative" or "radically abstract" and which in its very structure, syntax, and rhetoric cancels in advance the pseudo-mimeticism or photographocentric thought of standard philosophy. Laruelle's text on photography is in my view the key to the whole of non-philosophy. It makes clear that it is an exercise in a self-critical experimentation with the materiality of philosophical prose. As O'Maoilearca notes:

> Non-philosophy cannot be representational ... because that would once again virtualize or mix the Real with what is unreal. For immanence to be radical, it must not be *mixed* with any kind of transcendence, any reflection, representation or any decision as

to the nature of the non-philosophical ... The Real can neither be known nor even thought, but can only be "described in its axioms."[51]

As I have argued elsewhere, Laruelle proposes not an aesthetics to be decided by non-philosophy, but an *aesthetics of writing non-philosophy*.[52] Again as O'Maoilearca notes:

> For Laruelle, the establishment of a radically immanent philosophy, one which escapes transcendence cannot be achieved in and through traditional philosophy at all: it can only be instituted through a "non-philosophical" thought whose subject matter is the history of philosophy itself. This non-philosophy will thus appear similar to philosophy, but only because its raw-material is traditional philosophy.[53]

Non-philosophy thus "is not just a theory but a practice," notes O'Maoilearca, it "re-writes or re-describes particular philosophies but in a transcendental way."[54] Non-philosophical writing rigorously and scrupulously voids the decisionist imperative of standard philosophy and cancels the operativity of the capitalist principle of exchange and equivalence that underwrites the standard philosophical economy of thought. The turn to aesthetics here is in fact a turn toward the materiality of philosophical materials and to a conception of non-philosophy as a sensuous activity of making. For aesthetics is fundamentally a practice of the senses. I do not, however, mean to suggest that non-Marxism is mere word-play. But it is surely a *matter of words* and a *matter of making* with verbal materials a "rigorous" thought that is non-philosophical in the last instance.[55]

Non-Marxism is a "Stranger-subject"—stranger than we have known from philosophies of Marxism. It is estranged from the decisionist games of standard philosophy. For Marx, "estrangement" names the estranged relation between self and worker. This estrangement is wrought by commodified forms of work. But this moment of estrangement also (*pace* Henry) illuminates the radicality of the individual as that which cannot be seamlessly integrated into the logic of domination. The moment of estrangement is a painful realization that the world is unjust and must be changed. Non-Marxist theory clones and transforms the concept of estrangement to figure in non-figurative terms the "Stranger-subject" as the name for a subject who is rightly ill-adapted to the rigors of rationalized labor. But it also names a form or mode of writing philosophy—of working with philosophy as raw materials—in such a way that estranges them by rendering them strangely unworkable within the standard economy of knowledge production whereby the Real is exchanged for concepts and subordinated to them. Non-Marxism does not seek to put an end to alienation or estrangement. Only "the philosophically poised mind," notes Kolozova, seeks to "overcome the spit or alienation by way of assigning it a meaning."[56] Estrangement does not have a *philosophical meaning* for non-Marxism, but it is meaningful (painfully so). The non-Marxist, notes Kolozova, "affirms the grounding alienation" or estrangement "without ontologizing it."[57]

The labor of non-Marxist theory maintains and magnifies the estranging dissonance between philosophy and the Real. But in its estrangement, strangely, non-Marxism remains faithful to the radicality of the Real precisely insofar as it refuses to do what it axiomatically claims cannot be done, namely, to decide that which is always already decisive—the Real. The "*non-Marxist practice of Marxism*," writes Laruelle, "is destined to struggle against the 'particular interests' of philosophical systems desperately attempting to capture it and this can already be seen in Marx's work."[58] Non-Marxism remains faithful to Marx's "sojourn in philosophy" (*pace* Labica). It recognizes the necessity to work with philosophy but not to affirm its capitalist logic. Marx or Marxism after Laruelle will appear strange. But in that strangeness, it recalls the rightful violence of the Marxist tradition against the epigones of common capitalist sense. But is there nothing more to non-Marxism? What about the matter of political struggle? It is to this question that we turn in the next chapter.

3

Struggle

The aim of this chapter is to situate Laruelle's non-Marxist concept of struggle. Specifically, its aim is to situate *struggle in theory*. The reader might despair here. Why introduce *theory* into the question of non-Marxist struggle when non-Marxism aims at the liberation of Marxism from philosophy? Laruelle himself is keen to distinguish between philosophy and theory. The latter—understood non-philosophically—remains an important source of creativity and a vital source of resistance for the non-Marxist project. Laruelle writes that non-philosophy "produces *theoretical* and no longer *philosophical* thought."[1] This quote comes from Laruelle's *Theory of Identities* under the telling subheading: "Non-Philosophy is practiced in the manner of a theory."[2] The phrasing here is decisive. Non-philosophy theoretically is a certain form of practice. My argument is that this "practice" is a practice of struggle with philosophical materials. The question then is: what are the stakes of theoretical struggle in the non-Marxist conjuncture? This chapter seeks to illuminate this question by constellating the work of two of Laruelle's contemporaries, Louis Althusser and Mario Tronti. I read the names of Althusser and Tronti as proper names for two contending emphases in western Marxism of the mid-twentieth century: the primacy of theory (Althusser) and the primacy of political practice (Tronti). My wager is that Althusser's and Tronti's work proves useful for illuminating the stakes of Laruelle's work in light of the dynamic debate between the primacy of theory and the primacy of practice that electrified and divided the historical conjuncture that produced non-Marxism.

Theoreticism

Althusser's work commenced in earnest with the publication of two works in 1965: *For Marx* and *Reading Capital* (which he co-wrote with students). These two volumes introduced readers to a now familiar set of Althusserian concepts: "theoretical practice," "overdetermination," "symptomatic reading," "epistemological break," the "young Marx," and "theoretical anti-humanism," to name only a few. These terms are linked in the fabric of Althusserianism, but I want to focus on the first of these.

In *Reading Capital*, Althusser attempts (in part) to explain how it is that Marx was able to see why the question concerning the value of labor had gone unanswered by classical political economy. The classical school presumed that the market revealed the worth of things. Hence, if the price to reproduce labor is the subsistence cost of the laborer, then labor is worth a subsistence wage. But what Marx showed in *Capital*, argues Althusser, was that the classical theory displaced the question concerning the value of labor for the value of the subsistence of the laborer. Put simply: the classical school's theory of labor value is constructed around the wrong concept; laborer as opposed to labor power. What the classical political economists "called the 'value of labor,'" writes Marx, "is in fact the value of labor power, as it exists in the personality of the worker, and it is as different in its function, labor, as a machine is from the operations it performs."[3] Commenting on this passage, Althusser writes:

> The original question as the classical economic text formulated it was: what is the value of *labor*? Reduced to the content that can be rigorously defended in the text where classical economics produced it, the answer should be written as follows: *"The value of labor (...) is equal to the value of the subsistence goods necessary for the maintenance and reproduction of labor (...)."* There are two blanks, two absences in the text of the answer. Thus Marx makes us *see* blanks in the text of classical economics' answer; but that is merely to make us see what the classical text itself says while not saying it ... Hence it is not Marx who sees what the classical text does not, it is not Marx who intervenes to impose from without on the classical text a discourse which reveals its silence – *it is the classical text itself which tells us that it is silent*: its silence is *its own words*.[4]

Althusser is clear that "it is not Marx" who reveals the "silence" in the classical text, but rather Marx's *text* makes visible the blanks inscribed in classical political economy. Marx's *theory (not Marx the man) makes visible* that which was visible but which had gone unseen by classical political theory. Every effort here is made by Althusser to provide an explanation for the condition of possibility for Marx's insight without affirming the humanist concept of the individual subject of consciousness (genius or otherwise). Althusser does not theorize a visionary Marx, but a *particular visibility immanent to Marx's theory*. Any explanation that relies on an account of Marx's subjectivity, argues Althusser, ratifies the humanist concept of the "subject" and in so doing runs counter to what Althusser sees as the fundamentally anti-humanist logic of Marx's scientifically mature work. For Althusser, Marx's mature science is grounded on the concept of "class" whereas "subject" is a bourgeois-humanist concept immanent to the *ideology* of the liberal tradition. "Theory," for Althusser, makes the visible theoretically seeable. But this capacity to see is not rooted in the model of subject *qua* consciousness. "The sighting" at issue, writes Althusser, is not "the act of an individual subject, endowed with the faculty of 'vision' … the sighting is the act of [theory's] structural conditions."[5]

The above passage is arguably the most symptomatically stressed in all of Althusser's work for here his anti-humanist orientation is put under the most acute pressure as it attempts to grasp the revolutionary character of Marx's theory without ideologically reifying Marx the man. "Theory" functions as the displaced name for a-subjective agency. We can make this a little less abstract with a simple example. Anyone who has sat down to write a philosophical or theoretical paper has likely had the experience when suddenly the logic "clicks" into place and the paper "writes itself." Theoretical postulates "automatically" open certain conclusions and close off others. At the moment the paper "clicks," one is in possession of what is rightly called a theoretical "program" as the logic immanent to the theoretical exposition programmatically demands certain effects. Althusser's *theory of theoretical practice* aimed at grasping this agency internal to theoretical practice.

Laruelle draws on Althusser frequently in overt and covert ways. Althusser's concern for the status of theory or philosophy in Marx is resonant with Laruelle's concern to trace and critique philosophical effects within Marxism. Where their interests and concerns diverge, of course, is over the ultimate aims of their respective projects. Whereas Althusser attempts to decipher the philosophy of the "mature" Marx, Laruelle draws on the early Marx in order to radicalize what he sees as the fundamentally non-philosophical orientation immanent to Marx's theorization. But Laruelle agrees with Althusser that theory is not *reflective*, but productive. Althusserian "theory" like non-Marxism is a doing—a "practice." Laruelle might well have written these words by Althusser:

> [T]heoretical work is not an abstraction in the sense of empiricist ideology. To know is not to extract from the impurities and diversity of the real the pure essence contained in the real, as gold is extracted from the dross of sand and dirt in which it is contained. To know is to produce the adequate concept of the object by putting to work means of theoretical production (theory and method), applied to a given raw material. This *production* of knowledge in a given science is a *specific practice*, which should be called *theoretical practice—a specific practice, distinct that is, from other existing practices* (economic, political, ideological practices) *and absolutely irreplaceable at its level and in its function.*[6]

Like Althusser, Laruelle is concerned with the possibility of a science of philosophy in the last instance. But his perspective sharply diverges from Althusser over the status of science in the Marxian enterprise. "The theoretical system of Marxism," writes Laruelle, "is not only philosophical, it is also scientific but the science here plays a secondary role."[7] For Laruelle, the problem with Althusser's reading, which he commends as "rigorous," ratifies the secondary status of science in Marx. Precisely by trying to discover (or found) Marx's philosophy, Althusser marginalizes the scientific import of Marx's work. The concept of science in Althusser "remains abstract and ideological," notes Laruelle, because it is hedged in by "the general presuppositions ... of philosophy, not at all those of science alone."[8] Althusser himself later rejected his initial theoreticist orientation and tried to reestablish a *theory of theory* on a fundamentally political and partisan basis. This turn was precipitated by criticisms of his work voiced by numerous Marxists.

Althusser's Critics

Althusser drew the ire of a number of Marxists. E. P. Thompson, for one, notes in "The Poverty of Theory" that Althusser's theory of theoretical practice arrogates leadership of socialist struggle to an elite cadre of theorists whilst the working class is left to produce and do the fighting. The working class *does*, but the theorists *decide* the theoretical significance (or not) of their various doings. The philosophical significance of class struggle and the production of historical change is to be "obediently processed by graduates and research assistants," writes Thompson, safely ensconced behind the "emplacements of the École Normale Supérieure."[9] Thompson accuses Althusser of unabashed elitism and for affirming the capitalist division of labor between manual and mental production. A similar criticism is voiced with far more theoretical rigor by Jacques Rancière. In *Althusser's Lesson*, Rancière turns against his former teacher. Rancière indicts Althusser for producing a theory based on the presupposition of the inequality of intelligences. In his 2010 introduction to the republication of *Althusser's Lesson*, Rancière notes that "my book declared war on the theory of the inequality of intelligences."[10] Theoreticist thought is counterrevolutionary for it ratifies that workers should work (because that is all they can do) and theorists (those with philosophical training) should do the thinking. Contra theoreticism, "revolutionary thought must be founded on the inverse presupposition," writes Rancière, which acknowledges "the capacity of the dominated."[11] Rancière rebukes the Althusserian model of the revolutionary subject as a worker whose domination deprives him or her of the capacity to practice revolutionary thought. Rancière sums up Althusserianism with a swift and biting parody. Althusserianism says:

> [P]roduction is the business of workers, whereas history is too complex an affair for them, one they must entrust to the care of specialists from the Party and from Theory. The masses produce – and so they must, otherwise we scholars would have to do it … The masses should wait for the "theses" that specialists in Marxism work out for their benefit. Roll up your sleeves and transform nature; for history, though, you must call on us.[12]

Rancière's devastating and brilliant critique of Althusser exposes what might be called the *ideology of Althusserianism*. Althusser's (perhaps unwitting) affirmation of the capitalist division of mental and manual labor functions as an alibi to preserve and defend a dictatorship of intellectual aristocratism. Rancière draws a non-philosophical lesson from Althusser's teaching: radical philosophy itself (in certain of its practices) functions as a conservative ally for the defense of the very class system it challenges and resists. At the level of "theory," the struggle against class domination is silenced by the authority and authoritarianism of the decisionist pronouncements and theses of philosophical reason. But whereas Rancière seeks to correct Althusser's theoreticist deviation by recourse to workerist thought in the nineteenth-century archive primarily, Laruelle turns to a meta-theoretical strategy that seeks to institute and normatively defend democracy in thought. Democracy *in thought* or theory must "pass from the terrain of philosophy," writes Laruelle, to a concept of "theory rethought and reformulated as the intrinsic identity (without an epistemo-logical synthesis) of the science of philosophy."[13]

On Laruelle's identarian terrain—but an identity voided of philosophical unity—science and philosophy are treated equally as material for a scientific study of the constitution and effects of domination by philosophical reason. The "first possible form of democracy within thought," writes Laruelle, "is precisely what we call 'theory' qua the identity of science and philosophy, which equally plays a role in each part, meaning outside the domination of philosophy over science."[14] Science and philosophy are treated as equally insufficient to capture the Real as such. Laruelle intervenes in the internal politics of philosophy itself inasmuch as he levels science and philosophy down to materials to be reworked. Philosophers are non-philosophically redefined as material workers without *a-priori* privileged access to the Real of history.

Theory as Struggle

Althusser amended his views in the 1970s. He judged his theory of theoretical practice to be a "theoreticist deviation." Althusser confessed to his supposed failure to assert and defend the primacy of class struggle. His corrective was to subordinate theory to what might be called *the conceptual dictatorship of the proletariat*. It is the revolutionary class that makes history and is the condition of possibility for the production of revolutionary thought. Any philosophical schema that grants autonomy to theory displaces the primacy of class struggle by an idealist (read Hegelian) error. The theoreticist deviation denies the motor force of history *qua* the revolutionary class. Hence, Althusser attempted to "put things right" by "putting forward other propositions."[15] He tries: "Philosophy is politics in the field of theory."[16] On another occasion it takes this form: "philosophy is, in the last instance, class struggle at the level of theory."[17] Here the concept of "struggle" enters into the definitional frame of theory itself, suggesting that "struggle" both within and against theory is immanent to theoretical practice. This "struggle takes the form, proper to philosophy," writes Althusser, "of theoretical demarcation, detour and production of a distinctive position."[18] Althusser insists that "this [new] conception of philosophy as struggle implie[s] a reversal of the traditional relation between philosophy and politics."[19]

However, Althusser's "reversal" in large only intensifies his initial "theoreticist deviation" by intensifying the antagonistic relation between philosophy and politics whilst preserving the structure of the very problematic it seeks to topple. No slogan accomplishes this toppling no matter how intense, not even: "philosophy is fundamentally political."[20] Nor does this suffice: "To be a communist in philosophy is to become a partisan and an artisan of Marxist-Leninist philosophy: dialectical materialism."[21] To be a partisan and an artisan in philosophy is to side with a politically committed *practice of philosophizing*. "Althusser's attempt to correct his error," writes Gregory Elliott, "consisted in conceiving (and practicing) philosophy as a *political intervention in theory* and a *theoretical intervention in politics*."[22] But no matter how much Althusser prizes and privileges the radical and historically determinant character of class struggle, he cannot escape the structure that relates and divides philosophy from politics. As Althusser notes with reference to Lenin: "A single word sums up the *master* function of philosophical practice: 'to draw a diving line' between the true ideas and the false ideas."[23] But the drawing of the line between truth and falsity is drawn *within philosophy*. Althusser turns to Lenin's philosophical legacy to defend his theory as class struggle in theory.

In "Lenin and Philosophy," Althusser affirms Lenin's "Materialism and Empirio-criticism" in which Lenin radically reduces the whole history of philosophy to a non-history of the eternal recurrence of the struggle between materialism and idealism. Althusser freely admits that this affirmation of Lenin's thought risks embarrassment for Lenin's philosophy has none of the philosophical subtlety one expects of professional philosophical practice. Lenin is "intolerable" because he makes of philosophy a political practice.[24] Althusser writes:

The real question is not whether Marx, Engels and Lenin are or are not real philosophers, whether their philosophical statements are formally irreproachable, whether they do or do not make foolish statements about Kant's "thing-in-itself," whether their materialism is or is not pre-critical etc. For all these questions are and always have been posed inside a certain *practice* of philosophy. The real question bears precisely on this traditional practice, which Lenin brings back into question by proposing a *quite different* practice of philosophy.[25]

Lenin poses philosophy as a *quite different* practice of philosophy by practicing it politically. Lenin's reduction of philosophy to a non-history established through the eternal recurrence of the struggle between materialism and idealism casts philosophy as an eternal struggle. No "objective" means exist to settle this struggle. This is what is "intolerable." It is "intolerable" for philosophy to consider itself at bottom a battle for power and thus to see itself as "political" in the last instance. "[A]cademic philosophy cannot tolerate Lenin," writes Althusser, because it "cannot bear the idea that [it] ... might have something to learn from politics and a politician. And on the other hand, it cannot bear the idea that philosophy might be the object of a theory, i.e. of an objective knowledge."[26]

Science of Decision

Laruelle like the later Althusser takes the concept of struggle as determinative of his project. But he affirms that *philosophy itself* must be struggled against by a scientific practice that traces the workings and effects of Philosophical Decision. Laruelle's work is "intolerable" to professional philosophers because he, like the later Althusser, radically reduces philosophy to a materially, objective, or scientific object of study. But where he breaks with Althusserianism is in his defetishization of philosophical content in the name of studying philosophical material scientifically. Seen from Laruelle's vantage, Althusserian theory is determined by the Philosophical Decision that class struggle is of the order of the Real. Althusserianism names the struggle to situate philosophy as a determining operation in thought and political struggle.

Ted Benton argues that what is at ultimately at stake in Althusser's class struggle conception of philosophy is a struggle to establish and maintain a "tendency" in Marxian theory. Althusser's "materialist tendency" *qua* class struggle amounts to the "theoretical 'representation' of the world-view of the proletariat."[27] Althusser philosophizes this struggle as the struggle between capitalism (idealism) and communism (materialism). In the "last instance," writes Benton, what is at stake "in this tendency struggle is the hegemony of one or other world-views in contestation in the contemporary political class struggle."[28] What is at stake is either the hegemony of a worldview that, like capitalism, is founded on abstractions or a worldview established in fidelity to sharing material equitably by all (communism). But, as Benton points out, in order for Althusser to set up the hegemonic antagonism between materialism (communism) and idealism (capitalism) he "has to use the concepts of historical materialism."[29] That is, the reduction of philosophy to a "tendency struggle" between materialism and idealism is itself a materialist (communist) hypothesis. It is not a politically impartial view. It is an example of what Althusser calls *partisanship in philosophy*. Althusser admits that there is no way to insist on philosophy as struggle without struggling for this very conception. One cannot prove that philosophy is struggle (or class struggle in theory). Rather, this itself must be struggled for. Immanent to Althusserianism then is "the unprovability of philosophical tendencies" and "therefore of the essentially partisan character of philosophy."[30]

But how would this be struggled for beyond baldly axiomatic assertions? Moreover, how are we to take this axiom? Is it that philosophy *represents* class struggle in theory in the sense that it represents the interests of the exploited? Or, does it represent the interests of materialist philosophers? Is it precisely a class struggle *in theory*? Does "class" here signify a philosophical community as in a certain "class of philosophers?" If in the last instance the "real" political struggle is between proletariat and bourgeois, then are we to understand philosophy as a separate class struggle between materialists and idealists? Are materialists the analogue to the proletariat and idealists that of the bourgeois? What would allow for this analogy? What grounds it? Nothing. The silence of nothingness at the heart of the struggle tendency named "Althusserianism" is the silence of unprovability that speaks only in the mute gesture of Philosophical Decision.

In a remarkable essay, "Subjectivity without a Subject," Alain Badiou defends Althusser's political ontology of philosophy on the grounds that "what happens in philosophy is organically bound to the political condition of philosophy."[31] The problem here is that "the political condition of philosophy" *a priori* assumes that philosophy is conditioned by politics which is hardly a defense of Althusser. It is more like an echo. If politics, as both Althusser and Badiou insist, is not a subject, but a "process" then philosophy is not conditioned by a subject or a discipline but by the processes called "political practices." Hence, Badiou can write "genuine thought of process is possessed by those engaged in political practice."[32] "Genuine thought" belongs finally to the practices immanent to the "militant dimension" of politics.[33] But if militants are the real thinkers then what is it that academically trained philosophers can do? "What philosophy *is* able to do," writes Badiou, "is to record, in the unfolding of previously unseen political possibilities, the sign of a renewed 'thinkability' ... of politics *conceived on the basis of its own exercise*."[34] That is, philosophy's "exercise" becomes the practice of renewing what is "thinkable" in previous political practices. And because those practices "condition" philosophical practice then philosophy, on this model, amounts to the conceptualization of what is thinkable (and newly so) in concrete political practice and struggle.

Philosophy, Badiou tells us, is the act that decides what is thinkable in what first appeared as political practice. Philosophy for Althusser (as for Lenin before him) is a non-history of the repetition of the "same struggle" between idealist and materialist tendencies. As Badiou notes in *Philosophy for Militants*, "in philosophy, we have something invariant, something of the order of a compulsion to repeat, or like the eternal return of the same. But this invariance is of the order of the act, and not of knowledge."[35] What is this act? Badiou explains:

> Philosophy is not a theory, but a separating activity, a thinking of distinctions in thought. Therefore it can by no means theorize

politics. But it can draw new lines of partition, think new distinctions, which verify the "shifting" of the political condition.[36]

Philosophy's distinction is that it distinguishes. But precisely the same could be said for political practice. Do not militants make distinctions all the time, especially between friends and enemies? Badiou's defense of Althusser seems only to deepen the problem. To determine philosophy by political practice is to *decide* it as such. The struggle then is axiomatic: philosophy *must* be determined by the primacy of politics. But what of political practice? Is not thought also immanent to political practice itself? If it is then what would this entail for a theory of theoretical practice? This question drove Marxian theory of the 1960s toward "workerism" to which we now turn.

Thought Factory

Mario Tronti was the chief theorist of Italian *operaismo* (literally "workerism"). Workerism is founded on the axiom that workers, as a function of their immanent organization within the labor process, have the experience for anti-capitalist political practice and anti-capitalist struggle. Tronti's best-known collection of writings is *Workers and Capital*. The essays collected there are situated and conjunctural. They bear the marks of the embattled conditions of Marxian politics of the 1960s.

For Tronti, Marx established the possibility of a new politics via the establishment of the concept of "class" and "class struggle" understood in partisan terms from the side of exploited workers. Marx founded a form of thought that analyzed society through the *conceptualization of class* and by the partisan alliance of his thought with the working class. Marx's thought was of a composite kind: at once scientific and partisan; at once analytical and a form of struggle. Workerism sought to reestablish Marxian politics on the primacy of labor struggle.

Unique to Tronti's approach is the privilege he pays to an expansive conception of factory production. The factory is not only a place of work for Tronti; it is also a concept and a social logic that governs even late capitalist societies. The whole of society—including all those elements that are not immediately and materially tied to factory production—are nonetheless immanently *industrialized*. Tronti's *operaismo* or *workerism* places *political primacy* on production. But this is not economism. Tronti rejects the simplistic economistic model of labor versus capital. He argues that labor is *part of capital* (not its revolutionary other). "The working class," writes Tronti, must "materially discover itself to be *part* of capital if it wants to counterpose the *whole* of capital to itself. It must recognize itself as a particular element of capital if it wants to then present itself as its *general* antagonist."[37]

Tronti's theoretical wager is that the general condition of resistance should theoretically be based on the recognition that laborers are actually part of capital. Laborers are the means by which capital as value is created. Thus the struggle by workers against capital is actually a struggle within capitalism and therefore *against the conditions of possibility for the proletarian class itself*. "The collective worker stands counterposed not only to the machine, as constant capital," writes Tronti, "but to labor power itself, as variable capital. It has to reach the point of having as its enemy the whole of capital, including itself as part of capital."³⁸ The destruction of capital by worker-led resistance necessarily terminates in the destruction of the working class as conditioned by capital. "Labor should see labor power *as a commodity* as its enemy."³⁹ The mobilization of the working class is an imperative, but, for Tronti, this must begin "from within the production process."⁴⁰ The "production process" at issue for Tronti, again, is not simply that process that takes place within the walls of the factory; it is a social process that industrializes work, culture, politics, and so forth. Production processes take place within capital as a socializing force that subordinates all aspects of society to the rigors and metrics of rationalized production based on the maximization of productivity in the most economically efficient and profitable manner possible. The paradox is that this industrializing process by which the whole of society is transformed into a "factory" is hard to see since social labor empirically appears wholly unlike factory work.

Tronti writes:

> It is only apparently paradoxical that when the factory is a particular fact – even though an essential one – within society, it manages to maintain its specific traits distinct from the total reality. Yet, when the factory extends its control over the whole of society – all of social production is turned into industrial production – the specific traits of the factory are lost amid the generic traits of society. When the whole of society is reduced to the factory, the factory, as such seems to disappear.⁴¹

"Factory" names not only an empirical place of production, but the form of society immanent to capital in which all modes of production are measured by the metric of mass-scale commodity production. Balibar grasps the theoretical stakes of Tronti's formulation of workerism precisely. Tronti's theoretical novelty "has to do with the *centrality of the factory*," writes Balibar, "particularly the use of the professional hierarchy and the bargaining of wages."[42] The fact that all forms of work utilize some form of managerial control, and that the bargaining of wages is the only means of bettering working conditions within capital, indexes the hegemony of industrialization over all modes of labor and life under capital. Balibar notes that "factory" in this double sense—at once a place of production and the dominant form of social production—is what lends Tronti's work its theoretical force as it works equally-well for the analysis of factory-based and postindustrial economic forms. Balibar writes that for Tronti:

> There is the idea that, in contemporary capitalism ... the whole society becomes an extension of the capital-labor relations established within the factory, particularly the use of the professional hierarchy and the bargaining of wages as a way to regulate social conflicts in general. And this is combined with the idea that the factory is a *political arena*.[43]

Tronti rejects vulgar economism to be sure, but at the same time he affirms a certain productivism that connects the economic and political arenas. The issue here (and in this he is close to Althusser's theory of theoretical practice) is to frame *theory as a mode of production* rooted in "factory" conditions (in the two senses). The very mode of "factory" production provides the means for the *organization of political practice* proper to the conjunctural crisis of contemporary capital. Whereas for Althusser, the factory floor, like that of the classroom or the army barracks, are sites for the reproduction of capitalist ideology, Tronti sees these spaces as precisely spaces for modes of autonomous political production. These are sites of struggle and not only instances or sites of ideological (re)production.

Thought Production

If for Tronti, "factory" names the generalized condition of rationalized production in society and of society itself, then for Laruelle the question would be how to break out of this rationalized mode of thought production that regulates what we might call the *production of production*. That is, the question is not simply a matter of drawing workerist theses out of the lived conditions of the working class. Indeed, that solution in Laruelle's view could do nothing more than reaffirm the dominant supercapitalist logic. If true emancipation can only come about by the destruction of the "factory" conditions of social production, then, for Laruelle, what is needed is to think in "non-proletarian" terms (i.e., outside the terms established by capital itself). The proletariat, for Laruelle, is still too philosophical a concept. It is philosophically imbued with "the ultimate consistency of negation," writes Laruelle, that will reduce its own class and the whole of "class-being to zero-class."[44] We should rather consider a concept of the "non-proletariat," according to Laruelle, defined as *politically without-consistency* and therefore voided of any philosophically predetermined notion of consistency. Such a concept will function only politically and *not philosophically* in the last instance. Here there is a degree of convergence between Tronti and Laruelle inasmuch as both are committed to the struggle to wrench Marxian political practice free from the imperatives of Marxian philosophical doxa, even the doxa of Marx himself.

Autonomy of the Political

For Tronti, political struggle resistant to capitalism is (and must be) "autonomous" from the economico-philosophical sphere in the last instance. The theoretical gap that Tronti spots in Marx is precisely this gap between capitalist modes of production and autonomous modes of political practice. As Sara Farris notes, "for Tronti the 'political' gap in Marx's thought was due to the fact that historical materialism itself was 'a product of early capitalism.'"[45] The autonomy of Marxist politics is a necessity for Tronti to avoid the rigidification of Marxism into an a-historical ideological doxa. "Marxism has to engage with Marx not in his time," writes Tronti, "but in our own. *Capital* should be judged on the basis of *the capitalism of today*."[46]

Tronti's determinant *point of heresy* (*pace* Balibar) in Western Marxism is precisely his point of departure for an "autonomist" practice of Marxian politics. Tronti's key move is to radicalize the concept of historical materialism. To think as a historical materialist is to think firstly that "materialism" and "materiality" are historical concepts tied to specific conjunctural sites of struggle within the logic of domination by capital. To be faithful to Marx's historical method requires the capacity to reinvent materialism in light of the historical present. For Tronti, political practice must be thought from this "autonomist" standpoint founded on the procedures (but not the letter) of Marx's work. As Farris notes:

> Tronti's consideration that Marxists (with the exception of Lenin) did not formulate useful indications for understanding the functioning of politics and state ... increasingly led them to resort to non-Marxist political thinkers in order to fill the gap in Marxist theory. For Tronti, it was in fact this science, this "art" of politics, that the Italian communist intelligentsia had to grasp as their autonomous raison d'être, without any thought of merely deducing them from a study of the economic situation.[47]

Tronti supplements the concept of the "primacy of politics" in the work of Lenin and the later Althusser with the concept of *the autonomy of the political*. For Tronti, Marxian politics is the great unthought in both Marx and Marxism. Each had tried to think politics from the standpoint of the primacy of class struggle or, as in vulgar economism, its superstructural relation to the economic "base." Neither position allows for a conception of the autonomy of political practice. Workerism seeks a mode of thought structurally open to the possibility of autonomous shifts in political practice and in the composition of a politically effective class. Tronti's Marxism is open to the inventiveness of struggle; the immanent power to reinvent the very concept and practice of struggle in and through the *practice of politics*. As Steve Wright observes:

> [Tronti] came to reject a notion of class consciousness as the mere aggregate of each worker's *Weltanschauung*. Struggle, rather, was seen as the greatest educator of the working class, binding the

various layers of the workforce together, turning the ensemble of labor-powers into a social mass, a mass worker.[48]

Workerism rejects the Lukácsian line concerning the development of "class consciousness." Against this Hegelianized vision of struggle, workerism (at least in Tronti's formulation) came to be understood as a process of the composition of an autonomous and politically effective class rooted in the exploited conditions of industrialized life and labor. There are not classes prior to production, but also production processes themselves do not simply produce a revolutionary working class. To work as a workerist is to work toward the composition of a politically effective working class. Workerism theoretically opened the possibility for a fundamental retheorization of the concept of class in and through the process of struggle in the "social factory."[49] This is what Tronti means by fidelity to Marx's "procedure" rather than the letter of his texts. One has to first examine "real" conditions and their effects on class composition in order to invent political practices appropriate to them. Tronti notes in "What the Proletariat Is":

> Already back in his day, Lukács had set these imposing words of Marx's at the epigraph for one of his own later-disavowed youthful essays: "It is not a question of what this or that proletarian, or even the whole proletariat, at the moment regards as its aim. It is a question of what the proletariat is, and what, in accordance with its being, it will historically be compelled to do."[50]

Tronti here quotes the young (Hegelian) Lukács who is himself quoting Marx. The itinerary of the quotation speaks to the historical battle between idealism and materialism as it played itself out on the terrain of Marxian theory of the 1960s. The question here is not what the proletariat should do, but what it is. This question is a question of whether or not (and to what extent) the identity of the proletariat will be decided by idealist fiat or by the material practice of political struggle. Quoting Marx again, Tronti writes:

> The proletariat ... is compelled as proletariat to abolish itself and thereby its opposite, private property, which determines its existence, and which makes it proletariat. It is the negative side of the antithesis, its restlessness within its very self, dissolved and self-dissolving private property.[51]

Whereas for Lukacs "class consciousness" is the determinant point in economic and political struggle, for Tronti the "proletariat" is the name for a solidarizing intervention (and invention) born of political struggle against the conditions that make that very struggle necessary. The working class, for Tronti, is not something that lies in wait to be discovered by "consciousness," but a process of political invention that brings it into being.

Tronti expands the concept of the "proletariat" as he does that of the "factory." "Proletariat" and "factory" are not simply names for working-class revolutionaries and a place and form of labor. "Proletariat" and "factory" are social modalities that condition the possibility for *proletarianizing political practices* aimed at taking ownership of the means of (social) production. But when this happens it will necessarily entail the eradication of the proletarian class *qua* engine of capitalist value production. Hence the proletariat's struggle against capital is a struggle against itself. The proletarianization of struggle creates a political class whose victory will be its historical disappearance. What the proletariat is, for Tronti, then is that historical process that conditions the composition of a class subject which is marked by the political struggle waged within itself against that which conditioned its very possibility.

Marx Today

Balibar astutely calls Althusser's and Tronti's interventions in Marxian thought a "point of heresy" inasmuch as both Althusser's "theoreticism" and Tronti's "workerism" represent key departures from orthodox positions even as both (in different ways) claimed a fidelity to Marx's thought. Althusser and Tronti both returned to Marx via a certain structuralist orientation. Althusser was concerned to read Marx in light of immanent, intra-theoretical structures, whereas Tronti was concerned to read Marx in light of the structures of lived labor relations under capital. The "return to Marx" for each was marked by a turn to structural reading and radical formalization in order to scientifically and politically reclaim the relevancy of Marx's work in the shadow of the "revelations" of Stalin's Russia. A comparative reading reveals that workerism (Tronti) and theoreticism (Althusser)—two very different political and theoretical orientations—both required *something more* than the letter of Marx's texts despite each claiming to be the right reading. Whereas Althusser was primarily concerned to read Marx in order to establish (or complete) the philosophy of dialectical materialism, Tronti read Marx in order to formulate a workerist politics of the present. But Althusser and Tronti shared an underlying commitment to read Marx for the present. The commitment to read *Marx today* structured and determined the theoretical and political profiles of theoreticism and workerism. By the 1960s the question of the future of Marxism appeared to depend less on an innocent return to the reading of Marx than a formal investigation into the *conjunctural conditions for reading Marx philosophically (Althusser) and acting politically as a Marxist (Tronti)* at a time when the Fordist paradigm was just beginning to reach its limits. Both Althusser and Tronti understood that in this time of transition it was important to open Marxian research to actual developments in recent scientific and political practices to avoid the Scylla of Stalinist orthodoxy and the Charybdis of reformism.

Subject-in-Struggle

The question of struggle and its relation to Marxian philosophy and practice has been our focus in this chapter. I want now to illuminate the ways in which Laruelle extends, develops, but finally breaks with the dyadic structure of politics and theory in Marxian thinking of the 1960s as figured by Althusserianism, workerism, and its legacies.

Laruelle theorizes struggle neither as a "subject without a process" (*pace* Althusser) nor as the enunciative composition of the proletariat (*pace* Tronti) bound to bring about its own destruction. Laruelle instead "dualyzes" the theoretical practice/political practice split (or theoreticism-politics split) to reconstruct a theory of the subject as a struggle waged against both philosophical and capitalist abstraction or what again he calls "supercapitalism."[52] The "subject-in-struggle" names that process through which something is born in (and as) struggle against both the abstractions of capital and of philosophy, including Marxist philosophy. Laruelle writes:

> The subject [in-struggle] is, in his identity, a transcendental *function* of conjunctures, but never as this historico-essentialized fetish of the "Proletariat." And struggle also constitutes itself ... without the ontological consistency of the contradiction. Struggle is radically subjective in-the-last-instance, deprived even of the sociologico-worldly anonymity of "class" And the struggle is structured radically as unilateral "in-struggle" like one is "in-life" or "in-immanence."[53]

The subject-in-struggle is a process that arises in (and as) struggle against capital itself, but it also names that struggle to think against supercapitalism (philosophy plus capitalism), which is to say against all exchange-based modes of thinking *according to* the radicality of the Real in the last instance. The alternatives—subject as function of conjunctures (*pace* Althusser) and as a function of political articulation (*pace* Tronti)—are treated unilaterally as a duality without resolution. There is no synthesis to be found here for Laruelle. Rather, his aim is to radically "dualyze" the relation between philosophical and concrete political struggle by taking struggle as what Alfred Sohn-Rethel would call a "real-abstraction."[54] To privilege theory over concrete struggle (the theoreticist solution) is too idealist. But to place the primacy on the autonomy of political practice (the workerist solution) is a materialist solution still wedded to the dialectical problem of theory/praxis and therefore still too philosophical for Laruelle.

The error common to both workerist and theoreticist orientations is for Laruelle the error of philosophy writ-large. Laruelle clones and transforms the concept of struggle into "subject-in-struggle," which names the dual struggle against philosophy and capitalism. Laruelle describes the non-Marxist orientation as "a new science that takes in a unified way the unique object of political economy *and* philosophy, the capital-form *and* philosophy-form."[55] At every instant in which struggle is articulated against capital in the language of class (or other socio-economic categories), then and there the philosophy of (as) capital is reproduced. Non-Marxism wages its struggle on both fronts—against capitalism *qua* economic form and against capitalist thinking—through an immanent struggle with philosophical materiality. Here the question of the subject in its dual meaning is decisive. The "subject-in-struggle" names both the immanent condition of struggle within the philosophical tradition and the "generic" human who carries on this struggle and for whom this struggle is waged in the last instance.

The Generic Human

The generic human (and animal) does not exist as such under capital. Instead there exist only capitalist figures such as "worker," conceptualized under capital not as a physical body, but as set of economic indices of efficiency and productivity. What is physical and animal—that which can be destroyed or killed—is effaced by the automated logic of capital. As Kolozova observes:

> According to Marx, ... industrial production, in its materiality, which includes the human body and mind too, is part of the universal machine of capital and it is a self-sustained universe without the need of human skill to guide it ... The prime mover of the capitalist automaton ... is generalized Reason shaped by philosophical humanism ... Humans are the necessary conscious elements built into the automaton [of capitalism] so they can serve the function of conscious linkages of oversight of the automated operations. The worker is part of the process only to be used as a form of means of production, as part of the "fixed capital" or the material required for the machine (of capital) to endlessly circulate.[56]

Kolozova's brilliant intervention forces to the fore capitalism's relentless destruction of all that is physical, animal, and human. Kolozova rightly recognizes that capitalism has no interest in the physical lifeworld. She therefore astutely avoids the liberal claptrap that calls for a more humane capitalism—capital with a human face. From the perspective of capitalism, physical animal life (humans and non-humans alike) is not simply "devalued." No value except the abstract value of real or possible exchange exists in the eyes of capital. Physical life exists in capitalism only (where possible) as a set of economic indices. Contra Lukács, what is decisive is not simply that workers become "conscious" of their "class" position, but of their *dual positioning within the physical and the abstract* as determined by the real-abstraction of life under capitalism. In this respect, Laruelle's position intersects to an extent with that of Tronti's. But where the non-Marxist project diverges from Tronti's program is in its resistance to both the abstract machine of capital *and* philosophy.

Non-Marxism resists the abstract whether in its "capital-form" or "philosophical-form," but paradoxically this resistance requires (*pace* Labica) a "necessary sojourn in philosophy." Capital's constant conversion of the physical into the computable mirrors philosophy's conversion of life into idea systems (and ideologies). Non-Marxism resists the dematerialization of life at the hands of economic and thought systems that deny the radicality of the Real. The non-Marxist challenge is twofold: a challenge to capitalist abstraction is (always already) a challenge to philosophical abstraction because *capitalism is a philosophical system and not only a system of economic production*. Non-Marxism is a *subject of study* essentially determined by its struggle against the philosophy-form of philosophical Marxism and bourgeois thought. All philosophies, that of Marxism included, for Laruelle, are coterminous with capitalist logic by virtue of their acquisitive desire to take possession of the Real by (and as) concepts.

For Laruelle, capitalism and philosophy are structurally symmetrical: each is premised on the principles of exchange and equivalence. Further, each operates according to an idealized vision of a closed economy. Capitalism operates on the metaphysical premise that all qualitative differences can be converted into differences of quantity. Exchange means giving something and getting something of equal "value," but in a different form. Likewise, standard philosophy is premised on the idealized vision that any aspect of the Real (or the Real itself) can be exchanged for a concept adequate or equal to it. The discovery of this structural symmetry of capitalism and philosophy is a genuine discovery of the non-Marxist project. Laruelle writes:

> [C]apitalism is to material life what philosophy is to thought: a constitutive principle … The object of non-Marxism is not exactly

the capital form [of philosophy] alone ... but what can be called "thought-world" since that object is understood through its philosophy-form side, and the "capital-world" since it is understood through its economico-capitalist [side] ... Strictly speaking, its object is then instead the *world-form* that invariably designates the mixture of the philosophy-form [and the capital form].[57]

"Laruelle is ... quick to make philosophy and capitalism coterminous," writes Alexander Galloway, "the two are, quite simply, the same thing."[58] Standard philosophy operates by reducing the Real (including the reality of physicality) to a set of concepts determined by a hierarchy of "values." The struggle of non-Marxism is to mobilize the raw materials of Marxism against its imprisonment in the supercapitalist form. In this key respect, Laruelle rejects the Althusserian project for he does not think that the problem for Marxist science is that it lacks an adequate Marxist philosophy. "Like Althusser, Laruelle shuns the lingering abstractions that permeate Marx," writes Galloway; however, the problem for Laruelle is not "one of bad philosophy ... but an excess of philosophy."[59] For Laruelle, philosophy and capitalism are structurally isomorphic inasmuch as both are structured by normative principles of exchange and equivalence. They are also united by a shared aspiration to universalize their logics. "Just as philosophy is not just any thought whatsoever, but a fundamental pretension and authoritarian legislation over every other thought," writes Laruelle, "likewise we *must posit* ... capital as a uni-versal hypothesis" by reason of it pretension to be "*an encompassing-of-itself-and-every-other-economico-social-phenomenon.*"[60] Laruelle's clones the concept of the universal as "uni-versal," notes Anthony Paul Smith, "to emphasize its oneness and movement. In this case 'uni' refers to 'oneness' while 'versality' indicates movement (as in the French *vers* or 'toward'")."[61] What Laruelle calls the "curse" of philosophy and capitalism or supercapitalism lies in its pretension to universalize its authority to legislate over all other forms of knowledge production by reproducing the principles of exchange and equivalence as normative or given structures for thought.[62] The supreme belief that philosophy as a *conceptual economy*, like the economy of economics, dominates and subordinates every other form of life and thought by linking them in a chain of concepts fused at every link by the principles of exchange and equivalence.

The ideological task of non-Marxism is to think beyond Marxian and bourgeois concepts of class and consciousness. These concepts have been materially shaped by capitalism and idealism. We should be clear here. The concepts of class and political consciousness marked an immensely important turning point in the history of ideas and of anti-capitalist resistance. But one should not forget that Marxian categories and terms were derived from the remainders of idealist philosophy and from the system of capital to which Marx devoted his life to analyzing systematically. What Marx made thinkable was the political condition of the capitalist system as a social system contra the classical model of political economy that envisions not a social system, but an aggregate of atomized buyers and sellers confronting one another on the "open" market. Marxian categories are concepts fashioned to make capital politically thinkable. For Laruelle, the problem *after Marx* is not to analyze capital, but more fundamentally to develop *modes of non-capitalist theory* by rendering the principles of exchange and equivalence that underwrite the standard economy of philosophy inoperative.

The process of rendering philosophical materials inoperative in the standard sense aims to "force" this transformation of philosophical material in order to produce what Laruelle calls a "fore-(of)-thought" that negatively illuminates what cannot be decided but is radically decisive—the Real. Non-Marxism is faithful to the Real without deciding it philosophically. The Real is presented in the syntax of non-Marxism (and non-philosophy generally) as that which thought is *in and determined by*, but it is not presented as an *object of philosophical thought*. "Force" is the putting to "work" of object and argument in a form that is syntactically and strategically incompatible with the operation of Philosophical Decision and thereby faithful to the radicality of the Real in the last instance. But what else does non-Marxism do? Does it have anything to say about struggle beyond its struggle against philosophy in the name of the generic human? What of labor, revolution, and the ethics of resistance? What about praxis? It is to these problems that I now turn.

Non-Marxist Praxis

Laruelle calls for a re-theorization of the capitalist conditioning of labor power as a conditioning of the subject within the immanent struggle between the human (qua non-philosophical human) and its supercapitalist abstraction as labor power. It is the struggle within this structure that Laruelle terms "non-Marxist praxis." The non-Marxist notion of praxis is understood by Laruelle as the "practical force" of struggle immanent within the antimony of the human through its rootedness within the Real and its philosophical abstraction. Laruelle writes:

> *Practical force* ... is therefore the concept of the "subject" that is most human, the least "ontological" and least "capitalist," and the most foreclosed it is possible to be through ontology and capitalism combined. Obviously, it must be immediately understood as ... "in-struggle" in-the-last-instance, but an immanent struggle with the capital-world, and not a struggle by way of a transcendence interposed with the capital-world. This is the real kernel of the "proletariat" and of course "class struggle" in their strict inseparability.[63]

The real human—the human immanent to the Real—is as foreclosed to Philosophical Decision as the Real itself. The dual and antinomical positioning of the human *in-the-Real* and in the supercapitalist World constitutes the ground of "practical-force" and delineates the field of non-Marxist struggle against the combined logics of the capital-form and the philosophical-form. The struggle is that between what can be decided (philosophy) and that which is decisive (Real). The "real kernel" of what Laruelle terms the "non-proletarian" is that immanently lived reality irreducible to philosophical abstraction. But it also names a *class of cloned philosophical concepts* put to "work" to make intelligible the underlying structural struggle between the decided (philosophy) and the decisive (Real).

We can thus speak of "labor power" as the proper name for the abstraction of human physicality into a quantifiable store of capitalist production and as that power (or force) of non-Marxist thought that intervenes in the immanent struggle within the "subject" of capitalism and of philosophy. The struggle to think this dual and antinomical condition of labor power as subjection to capital on the one hand, and as the force of non-philosophical thought against the capital World (and its philosophical double) on the other, is ultimately the struggle to produce a science of the capital-form and the philosophical-form. As Kolozova notes in reference to Marx:

> In order to arrive at a scientific account of humanity one needs to posit it axiomatically in a way that is fundamentally different if not opposite from the one that defines philosophy: the real and the real of humanity are in the last instance determined by matter or physicality and praxis, and, in giving an account of them, the thinking subject submits to the real rather than to any philosophy. Such is the position of Laruelle's non-philosophy but also of Marx: "The production of ideas, of conceptions, of consciousness, is at first directly interwoven with the material activity and the material intercourse of men, the language of life." ... The axiom at issue proffers a sufficient postulation of a post-philosophical project of formulating a method of human sciences.[64]

The human sciences in a non-philosophical register would axiomatically proceed from the postulation of the human as *in-the-Real* and thereby beyond the reach of Philosophical Decision or reduction. These sciences would also take the operations of philosophical capture as capitalist ideologies to be demystified in the name of what Marx calls the *language of life* or what Laruelle nominates as the *syntax of the Real*. This would be a *theoretical science* aimed at capturing the modes and methods of the pseudo-capture of the Real by philosophical and capitalist forms. This science begins with a formal reduction of philosophies of equivalence and exchange to raw material made ready for their reproduction into non-philosophical (and non-capitalist) forms. This science (perhaps still to come) will have been a non-proletarian science. Let me unpack this further.

Whereas the proletariat is a philosophical category derived from the capital-form, the non-proletariat is that "subject" constituted in and as "struggle" against the capital-world *and* the philosophical abstractions that structure it. Let me be clear on one point here. Laruelle's non-Marxism is not as it might otherwise appear a discourse that posits a two-sided structure—the real struggle and the philosophical struggle—but is instead a "unified" theory that takes as its axiom the non-exchangeability of concept (of struggle) and real (struggle). We need to be clear here that by a unity of struggle (against capital and philosophy), Laruelle means something quite different than "praxis" as traditionally conceived or other amphibological admixtures. At issue is not the blending or synthesis of theory and practice, but a radical non-exchangeability of the two determined in the last instance by the Real and not its conceptual double. The non-philosophical "struggle" then is to think the relation between Marxist theory and political practice in terms of the non-closure of this problematic as itself symptomatic of a structural deficit in the languages and operations of standard philosophy.

Ethics of Struggle or Victimology

Non-Marxism might appear at first glance as hopelessly hermetic. It can appear cutoff from urgent theoretical problems of Marxist theory and from equally urgent matters of political struggle. Indeed, it might appear solely as an arcane metaphilosophy. The non-Marxist sojourn into the obscure corners of Marxist theory might leave one asking: what is the point? Indeed, one might say there is no point especially if one rejects Laruelle's axiomatic starting points concerning the identity of standard philosophy and its conceptual insufficiency. Finally, one might be excused for not reaching the conclusion that Laruelle does about philosophy, namely, that it violently violates the always already prior conditioning of the Real by subordinating it to philosophical reason. But even if one does, this can appear to be a rather academic problem as compared to the facts of hunger, homelessness, mass incarceration, state-sponsored racism, colonialism, and other structural and systematic forms of oppression. But there is an ethical horizon in which non-Marxism struggles. It struggles in the *name of the victim*. I turn now to Laruelle's "victimology" before returning to the problem of struggle and the radicality of the Real.

Laruelle's political ethics is focused on what he calls "Victim-in-person," which is a "formal symbol" that stands for those who have been destroyed by the violence of abstraction whether exercised in the flesh or in the mind.[65] It is paradoxically a "formal symbol" for a reality that is anything but merely formal. It names lived terror. It formally assigns a name to the violence that has been done in the name of politics and reason. Here we see why Laruelle has been such a critic of Badiou.[66] He cannot forgive Badiou's fidelity to Maoism in the face of its victims nor can he abide Badiou's attempt to rescue the idea of Maoism from the historical wreckage wrought by its political realization. But his critique is not restricted to Left philosophy. He also indicts Martin Heidegger too. Indeed, he places Badiou and

Heidegger on the same ethical plane. These figures name a "passion for the real" (*pace* Badiou) that victimized many by turning persons into philosophical abstractions subordinated to a totalizing philosophical program. Laruelle writes:

> Heidegger, on the one hand, calls for and celebrates the advent of the principle of the German people as order and will on the spatio-historical stage [i.e. he calls for a philosophy in line with Nazism]. Badiou, on the other hand, at the end of the twentieth century, reinstates the Maoist order in conceptual philosophy by a resurrection of dialectal materialism, which is accompanied by a philosophy of the decision and ethics of fidelity restricted to the trace of the event. These are both ... thoughts of force ... They admire only the founding heroes ... and have nothing but scorn, denial, or at best indifference for democracy and victims.[67]

Laruelle sees an intimate relationship between philosophy and political violence and victimization. To think of persons as political abstractions—the mass, the enemy, allies, working class, revolutionaries, the people—is to deny their radical rootedness *in-the-Real*. Thought victimizes human beings and animals alike whenever it conceptualizes them as abstractions or converts them into mere indices of economic or political life. There is a structural intimacy between Laruelle's cloned concept of the Real and the Victim-in-person. Both are formal names for what abstract formalization forgets, namely, that the Real and victims can only be decided by an act of thought-violence that subjugates them to the dictatorship of philosophical concepts. But is there not an inconsistency here? Is not the term "Victim-in-person" precisely an abstraction of real victimization? Indeed, Laruelle's victimology project is presented within what he calls a "general theory of victims." Is not a "general theory of victims" precisely a philosophical generalization of the sort that Laruelle claims victimizes the lived reality of victimization?

Laruelle defends his project. He writes, under the heading "theoretical preparation and precaution" that to "ensure its rigor and efficacy, a general theory of victims must expunge many useful or asserted nuances and organize itself around several fundamental concepts."[68] But what is key is that what Laruelle calls "victims 'in themselves'" are excluded from this general theory. Victims are not the object of his general theory. Rather victimology is a science that diagnoses the violence done by philosophies that claim to know and speak for the reality of victimization. This "general theory" axiomatically stipulates that "it is impossible … to speak of victims 'in themselves' the way common sense, the media, and thus philosophy speaks of them," writes Laruelle, "assuming that this object, its production, its affects, and its tasks are well known."[69] Victim-in-person is a "generic" name or "formal symbol" for what precedes every philosophical abstraction concerning not only victims but all human and animal beings. "The generic orientation, human but not humanist or philosophical," writes Laruelle, "is centered on the notion of 'Man-in-person' and 'Victim-in-person,' notions meant to avoid the classic definitions of man such as 'rational animal,' 'political animal,' 'metaphysical animal,' and so on."[70]

Victim-in-person is also (and more fundamentally) a formal symbol for all the ways in which standard philosophy in its academic, political, economic, and social manifestations convert the lived reality of human beings into "problems" that it claims to have the power to solve because it truly knows what is to be human. Victimology calls this presumption into question and tracks the diverse ways in which philosophy (in Laruelle's broad sense) turns lived reality into abstractions and thereby violates its radical alterity. Victimology is "a generic process" that necessitates "reduction" not of the human, but the *philosophical reduction of the human.* "It is a question of founding ethics," writes Laruelle, "on the unlocalizable and sometimes unidentifiable victim rather than on the metaphysical or philosophical force that took him for profit or loss."[71]

Laruelle's ethics (or non-ethics) intersects with his non-Marxist project. The victim of philosophy is accorded a profit/loss status. The victim is judged in terms of how it profits or fails to profit a philosophical position or posture. The victim for philosophy (and *of* philosophy literally) is used by philosophy as a means to defend or prosecute metaphysical, political, juridical, or simply philosophical projects. Non-Marxism is oriented toward what these practices forget: the radicality of the Real and the lived realities of victims. It offers no recommendations for what is to be done. But this is not quietism. It battles against the logic of abstraction *in the name of the Victim-in-person* without concretizing the victim into a figure of philosophical self-justification. The point is that to use human beings as philosophical or political props is violent and it is against this violence that non-Marxism wages its ethical struggle. To practice non-Marxism is to ethically disavow philosophical knowledge of the victim. There is then an ethical practice at the heart of non-Marxist theory. But this immanent practice inside its theoretical façade strains the commonsense way in which the relation between theory and practice has been traditionally considered in the Marxist canon.

Practice of Non-Marxist Theory

For Laruelle, theory and practice are *in-the-Real* and from this vantage—what Laruelle calls "Vision-in-One"—there is no relation to speak of between the two terms. One might provisionally speak of a relationality between theory and practice. But one cannot, according to Laruelle, speak of a relationality relative to the Real. The Real is non-relational as it is axiomatically, for Laruelle, One and radically prior to the event of Philosophical Decision and scission. We can postulate the Real as without relation, but we *cannot think this without recourse to the relational and decisionist languages of philosophy*. The non-Marxist solution is to take philosophical language as raw material and not as the truth of the Real. Thus, it thinks within the Marxian philosophical vocabulary, but according to the radicality of the Real in the last instance. As Laruelle notes:

> It is useful to distinguish between the practical, the theoretical, and the pragmatic and to set out their exact relations. Theory and practice form, for example, a duality that Marxist philosophy draws upon, sometimes from one side, sometimes from the other, by way of a typical philosophical balance. It [this philosophical balancing act] cannot be avoided except through its determination by the Real itself.[72]

The philosophical problem of the relation of theoretical practice to political practice "cannot be avoided" since our inherited languages and logics compel us to think this question as a problem of relationality. But from the perspective of "Vision-in-One" theory and practice are immanent to the Real. But because this immanence cannot be thought non-Marxism is forced to operate within the philosophically dichotomous tension between theory and practice. It offers no sublation or dialectical resolution to this tension. Rather, it reworks the problem of the tension by reading it as symptomatic of the antimonies of philosophical reason. Both the matter of the actuality of practice and the theory of theoretical practice are left open and available to invention within the non-Marxist conjuncture. And it remains committed to salvaging materials from the worlds of practice and theory in order to constitute and support a practice of thought that constitutively decides against the imperatives of Philosophical Decision on both the matter of practice and theory.

The practice of non-Marxist theory is the practice of Marxian thought otherwise than that determined by philosophical Marxism. As noted this practice makes of Marxism what Laruelle nominates as a "Stranger-subject."[73] In the particular context of the non-Marxist project, the "Stranger-subject" is twofold. It refers at once to a stranger Marxism than we have known and to the "subject" that exercises that newly estranging resistance to dominant philosophical forms of Marxism. Stranger-subject cannot be conceptualized beyond the resistance it exercises against the supercapitalist principle of exchange and equivalence. To give it a positive consistency would convert it from a stranger into an intelligible subject inscribed within the supercapitalist structure of domination. Non-Marxism ethically remains estranged from the *topoi* of familiar modes of philosophical Marxism. Yet at the same time it remains in touch with them precisely so as to smuggle out raw materials with which to clone and recode the Marxian program. The non-Marxist must be a stranger to familiar schools of philosophical Marxism, but to be a stranger in the house of philosophical Marxism is to still be in the house if not the family. Indeed, there has always been a "clandestine" Marxism that has haunted its official postures and historical stances. Witness the Marxist history of denunciations and accusations of heresy. What is this history if not the history of persecuting the stranger in the house of Marxism? The stranger must be close enough to even be recognized as a stranger. "What makes someone a stranger," writes Smith, "is not a totally unrecognizable nature, but a commonality that does not quite fit into one's own framework for making sense of a certain field of experience."[74]

Stranger-subject (at once of non-Marxism and a non-Marxist) constitutes a theoretical practice of resistance resistant to the theoretical practice/political practice split. Laruelle writes:

> This gives back to the Leninist maxim ("without revolutionary theory there is no revolutionary practice") its full meaning if only it is the "revolution" (belonging to the same form of thought-world, of capital, of history and philosophy reunited) that must be suspended by the "subject" and his uni-lateral action over the World. In this way the concept of "theoretical struggle," the introduction of the division of classes within theory must also … be treated as a symptom.[75]

Only in the struggle against the thought-world of supercapitalist structures and normative reproductions of the principles of exchange and equivalence can a *theoretical revolution* be carried out in which class division and struggle will no longer appear as the motor-force of history, but as symptomatic of the ordering of the world and thought according to the logic of supercapitalism. We have class theory because we have a thought-world that taxonomizes subjects into economico-political units. It is this logic that the Stranger-subject of non-Marxism struggles against and in only this struggle can it be said to exist.

Non-Marxism appears strange and as a stranger in a world of Marxisms derived from the capital-world and determined by the decisional structure of the standard philosophical-form. Non-Marxism's appearance as stranger (or "Stranger-subject") itself clones the originary strangeness of Marxism's first appearance in the capital-world. Non-Marxism is not so much a "return to Marx," but a return to Marxism's originary strangeness; its awkward incompatibility with the world of conceptual and material exchange. As Laruelle notes:

> Marxism was [...] like a Stranger who neglected to announce his arrival who paid hardly any attention to the bearers of good and bad news. Only a clandestine Stranger can arrive and by this arrival resist the Evil Demon of capitalism that never stops deforming subjects through the force of regulations and deregulations, through legal means and illegal means, through the perversion of norms and exceptions, through the redress of humiliations, and the enriching of exploitations.[76]

Only a "clandestine" or "heretical" Marxism—a non-standard Marxism—can arrive again (or return) as Marxism first arrived. Marxism's arrival as a haunting specter, as the *Communist Manifesto* famously announces, was unannounced. Its arrival resisted rational temporalities—newly born it was dead on arrival—which is to say it's coming was of the real future as Jacques Derrida taught us.[77] The future is the *to-come* of the Other of temporal predictability whose coming cannot be predicated or predictably rationalized. The future, contra the ideology of the "futures market," is irrational. A non-Marxism in the making, still to arrive unannounced, is by necessity a Marxism open to a future and which can still surprise again all those who operate within a still too philosophically rationalized Marxism itself derived from the philosophies immanent to the capital-world that produces and legitimates suffering as only rational. The struggle of non-Marxism is to preserve the possibility of an irrational and even impossible future within the present structure of enforced economic "reason." Non-Marxism will have been that *"practice of Marxism … destined to struggle against the 'particular interests' of philosophical systems desperately attempting to capture it."*[78]

The Question of Primacy

Non-Marxism is historically and conceptually situated neither on the side of the primacy of theoretical practice (Althusser) nor that of political practice (Tronti). Rather, it is determined by a decision *not to decide the question of primacy* for this question is still too philosophical. The entire tropology of theory and practice in the Marxist tradition is ultimately a *philosophical problematic* whose solution necessarily entails a philosophical solution and hence guarantees in advance the answer to the question that the question of primacy raises. At the same time, this question itself is the site of the immanent struggle with (and within) philosophy that "cannot be avoided" since non-Marxism is forced to think the question of the struggle against philosophy *using philosophy as its own raw material.*

Hence, the question that we have presented in terms of the proper names of Althusser and Tronti returns as the necessary conditions for a non-Marxist practice of Marxism inasmuch as such a practice will begin from the question of primacy reduced to the raw material necessary for thinking Marxism otherwise than philosophically. Non-Marxism affirms the Althusserian thesis concerning the necessity of the autonomy of theory whilst it affirms the necessity of concrete struggle in order to preserve all that is humane in an inhumane system. It requires a workerist impulse aimed at putting to work anew the question of primacy by treating it as a symptom of philosophical reason. The question of the primacy of theoretical practice or of political practice—of theoreticism or workerism as the true name of struggle—is itself the symptomatic remainder, which, despite its philosophical deformations, spells out the unified immanence of "in-struggle" as determined by the Real in the last instance. In the next chapter, we will examine what forms non-Marxism might take.

4

Impossibilization

This chapter examines what the introduction of the "non" into Marxism entails for thinking in non-capitalist terms. The encounter between non-philosophy and standard Marxism forces to the fore the non-exchangeability and non-equivalence between philosophical concepts and the Real. The chapter situates this non-capitalist gap via a reading of Laruelle's debt to structuralism in the formulation of the axiom of philosophy *qua* Philosophical Decision. It then traces how this axiom determines Laruelle's cloned concept of the "finite individual" or the radically "ordinary" individual of non-philosophical life. This leads then to a comparative reading of non-standard Marxism's insistence on the non-commutability of concept and Real with that of Adorno's project of negative dialectics. This comparison functions to conceptually clear the way for a more situated and grounded explication of Laruelle's project to *impossibilize* philosophical Marxism.

Philosophical Decision as Structuralist Judgment

Ian James rightly argues that non-philosophy is indebted to structuralism. James's reading is sourced in Laruelle's axiomatic claim that every philosophy is marked by a single *structural* invariant that Laruelle names Philosophical Decision. What postdeconstructive "philosophy does is pose," writes James, "an immanence to be known on the one hand (the real, being, existence) and ... [a] transcendence of a figure, concept, or representation on the other."[1] The concept of the Real is thereby split in two between philosophical thought and reality and then sutured together in the form of a system of concepts and decisions on the Real. James continues:

> [T]he structural invariant of philosophy suggests that philosophy will always repeat its deep structure as philosophy, whatever the form it may take – whether it be a full-blown metaphysics or ontology; any form of idealism, rationalism, positivism, empiricism, or naturalism; or destructive or deconstructive antimetaphysics or forms of skepticism and relativism. This is not so much because of what philosophy says of being, or how it says or speaks of being. Rather, it is so because it is positioned from the outset in what Laruelle calls the philosophical decision.[2]

Standard philosophy's decisions on the Real collectively constitute the *invariant structure* (or *invariant gesture*) that determines *philosophy as philosophy*. And this is precisely what makes Laruelle's judgment on standard philosophy a specifically structuralist judgment as I will show below.

Structuralism is in disrepair. Poststructuralism—itself marketized and bastardized—has entirely distorted the structuralist project. Damned as "totalizing" and stricken with "science envy," no one today can innocently say "I am a structuralist." Careful critics and intellectual historians know better, but the popular image of the structuralist as a failed scientist of the humanities has been hard to shake.[3] This gross misrepresentation of structuralism has also consequently damaged understanding of the "post" of "poststructuralism." The "post" should not be taken (as it frequently is) as a rejection of structuralism so much as a continuation and problematization of its general concerns. For example, the poststructuralist emphasis on challenging (or decentering) the concept of the sovereign subject as an *a priori* center or locus of meaning was itself already established in the structuralist orientation as is evident, for example, in the anti-authorial criticism of Roland Barthes or the anti-humanist reading of Marx by Althusser.

Vincent Descombes argues that structuralist analysis, contra the popularly held view, is not a totalizing mode of thought. The popular view that structuralist analysis requires a conceptualization of the analytical object's relation to a given "whole" or "total" system is flatly wrong. Structuralism is not concerned with totalities. This is precisely how it is different from standard philosophy. "Properly speaking there is no definable structuralist philosophy," writes Descombes, "such as might be opposed, for example, to the phenomenological school. 'Structuralism' is, after all, only the name of a scientific method."[4] Indeed, as I will later show, this aspiration to move from a humanistic study of the humanities to a "science" of the humanities is another point of affinity between structuralism and non-philosophy. But for the moment, I want to lay out Descombes's argument concerning the identity of the structuralist method in order to prepare the ground for a comparative analysis of non-philosophy and structuralism.

Descombes quickly dispels the myth that structuralist analysis proceeds by relating a given object (text or institution) to a total system (linguistic, political, social, etc.). This myth (a strong term in structuralist literature itself) was reproduced through countless introductory texts and popular study guides made in the wake of the poststructuralist turn. Descombes writes:

> If reference is made to the numerous Introductions to Structuralism available on the market, the following answer to the question of structural analysis which we are considering here will often be found: that the method of analysis is structuralist when meaning, in the object analyzed, is taken to be dependent on the arrangement of its parts. In short, the structuralist is held to have realized that an element may not be isolated from its context and that "everything is linked." This definition, restating in effect the perennial definition of the "framework" so dear to the schoolmasters, is clearly inadmissible.[5]

Why is it "inadmissible?" Because if one holds that "everything is linked" then analysis (structural or otherwise) is impossible. To analyze necessitates the isolation of a discrete set of elements. Structuralism is concerned to show how *specific operations* of thought (in language) are isomorphic across a number of domains. "Structure," writes Descombes, "is precisely that which holds good in an isomorphism between two sets of contents."[6] For example, a structuralist analysis of "confession" would isolate those elements of its structure—truth-telling, interiority, conscience, and so on—and isolate those elements that are isomorphic across religious, juridical, and perhaps literary fields. The point is that the analysis of the elements and their isomorphic features are analytically self-limiting rather than totalizing. Descombes writes:

> What is structured is not the thing itself, as literary criticism often imagines (so much so that on occasion it will draw attention to the structure as a feature of originality in the work under study), but the set of which this thing may be considered as one *representation*, in comparison with other sets. This is why structuralism moves from the structure to the model; it reconstructs or reproduces the given that it sets out to analyze.[7]

The object of study—text or institution—is held to be a possible "representation" or "model" of a set of invariants. Structural analysis then proceeds by *producing a model of this model* (or representation). Structuralism produces a model that models (or represents) the structural invariance found across an isomorphic set of relations. Laruelle's axiom that philosophy (Marxist or otherwise) is defined by Philosophical Decision is a structuralist axiom for it holds that the decision on the Real is the invariant element that links all philosophical practice.

Laruelle's non-Marxist work takes as given that Marxist philosophy is marked by the invariant structure of Philosophical Decision. The history of standard Marxist philosophy is a series of decisions on the Real: class struggle, historical materialism, consciousness, and so forth. Every attempt to clarify (or produce) Marx's philosophy reproduces the structure of philosophy's decisionist imperative. Laruelle writes:

The drive to make Marx intelligible, of making him acceptable according to the philosophical norms of acceptability, has led to completing him instead of un-encumbering him, of taking away from him his postulates which are useless for the definition of his essence and which are all specific and regional postulates, of the conditions of *universal capitalism* … If the "philosophical" problems of Marxism have a philosophical origin or cause, it will suffice to resolve them by determining the ensemble of its apparatus through the radical immanence of the Real.[8]

Laruelle's structuralist axiom of Philosophical Decision functions as the operative hinge for his reading of Marx as raw material for thinking beyond the invariant limits of philosophy. Non-Marxism seeks to find and invent experimental ways to disencumber Marx of his philosophical trappings. On Laruelle's reading, Marx's *Capital*, for example, reproduces the structurally invariant concepts of acquisitiveness immanent to supercapitalism, which is to say it is still too philosophical. Laruelle instead opts to follow not Marx's texts, but Marx's example, namely, that of a *non-philosopher* who used philosophy and a *non-economist* who used economics as raw materials to think against the domination of life by abstraction (philosophy) and exchange (economics). Laruelle writes:

Marx used philosophy without being (entirely and spontaneously) a philosopher. He used science without being (entirely and spontaneously) a scientist. Neither idealism nor positivism, but two paths that form only one: not dialectically or according to some other synthesis of deviations so as to form a kind of orthodoxy, but in an immanent manner through an identity of which we will say that it is *cloned* by the Real.[9]

Here again we see Laruelle's structuralist orientation come into view. Non-Marxism, like structuralism, operates *like philosophy without being philosophy proper* and *like science without being science proper*. Indeed, there is something definitively improper about non-Marxist thought (which is close to Marx) for it operates in the house of philosophical-capitalist abstractions in a way that refuses the rules of the abstraction game. Non-Marxism follows Marx by utilizing knowledge fields for ends that are non-instrumental. The object of non-Marxism is the structural invariants of a "world-form," of which capitalism and standard philosophy are models or representations. Laruelle writes:

> The object of non-Marxism is not exactly the capital-form alone or the history-form [i.e., historical materialism which is to say "philosophy"], but what can be called the "thought-world" since that object is understood through its philosophy-form side, and the "capital-world" since it is understood through its economico-capitalist side instead. Strictly speaking, its object is then instead the *world-form* that invariably designates the mixture of the philosophy-form and a regional content X [capitalism for example].[10]

In other words, the object of non-Marxism is the structure of invariance isomorphic between philosophy and a regional X such as economic reason, political ideology, party line, and so on. The relational structure binding philosophy to this X is structured by Philosophical Decision which predetermines that modes of *conceptual exchange* shall govern the life of thought and subordinate the living to dead abstractions. Laruelle's critique of abstraction resonates with Kolozova's profound intervention that demonstrates that capitalism and philosophy strive to substitute the physical with the speculative, but in ways that always fail. These failures are all too visible in what urban planners like to call "blight": homelessness, check-cashing stores, pay-day loan facilities, and all the other "signs" of what happens to physical life under the brutal reign of capitalist abstraction.

Finite Individuals

Supercapitalism's immanent drive is to make all things quantifiable under the logic of exchange. That which cannot "work" within this system is not permitted to exist. Death, physical or social, is visited on those who cannot "cope" in a "competitive" world. They are turned into diasporic waste found in the streets, prisons, detention centers, factory farms, and "bad" neighborhoods. Refugees from the capitalist thought-world surround on every side even while they are rendered invisible. They cease to be "counted" in job statistics. They are hidden behind thick walls. They are buried in discourse or else discursively transfigured into false monsters to justify the continuance of an inhumane world. These spectral traces haunt the supercapitalist imaginary. They are the consistently disavowed yet embodied reminders of the failures of a system that is persistently exonerated in the court of "professional" opinion. Our bankers and establishment economists sing the praises of our system or say that it is better than the "alternatives" or simply that there is "no alternative." Yet, of course, there is an alternative world. This alternative world is no utopia. It already exists in those other spaces, heterotopia as Foucault called them, that lie in the crevices and margins of sanitized and enforced social and political "normalcy." Laruelle invites us to think from the side of the minoritized for whom the State, power, and authority appear as the out-of-reach margin. This point of view prizes what Laruelle in *A Biography of Ordinary Man* calls the "finite individual."[11]

Laruelle defines the "finite individual" as the proper name for a mode of human (and other animal ways of being) that is uncountable according to the infinite calculus of monetized and conceptualized exchange under supercapitalism. The individual under the reign of supercapitalism is infinite—infinitely exchangeable and infinitely conceptualizable—which is only to say that there are infinite ways to "figure" it. By contrast, Laruelle's figure of the finite individual cannot be identified by the ruses of a philosophy of the subject, nor by a political ideology of the collective, nor by the principle of speculative exchange that underwrites capitalism and philosophy alike. The finite individual is *without history* inasmuch as it cannot be given a history that would not automatically be in some measure philosophical, political, social, or economic, and which would therefore convert it back into a transfinite subject which it is not. Any attempt to think the individual in philosophical terms transfigures it into a figure of infinite figuration. Simply put, we cannot conceptualize the finite individual under supercapitalist terms without infinitizing its finitude and thus destroying its actuality. Laruelle writes:

The actuality of the radically finite [individual], that which permits it to say "I," has no historical dimension: only political and philosophical Authorities interpret through extension and intensity, through activity and power, the impenetrable secret that is not of this [capitalist] World. A historical figure of man fades away in the same movement in which it is born, but man, the actual subject, [or the finite individual], is without figure. Were it not for philosophical and historical smugness, there would be no figure of man, and no part of him, at least of his essence, would be destined to fade like a ripple, die like a wave, pass like a river. History is an undertaking of auto-liquidation that sings the glory and the toughness of man.[12]

Laruelle here is riffing on Foucault's well-known passage in *The Order of Things* in which he declared that historically "man" was in a period of vanishing "like a face drawn in the sand at the edge of the sea."[13] Laruelle's covert critique of Foucault posits that it is precisely *historical thinking* that makes it possible to *figure* man *or* to make him "fade like a ripple." These are merely two sides of the same *philosophical* coin. To figure the individual—as "man," "human," "subject," and so on—are merely so many possible figurations in an infinite array of possible speculative abstractions. What must be thought is the individual without figure, without history, without story, entirely "ordinary" and invisible.

The concept of the ordinary, real, embodied, physical human—not the human of infinite philosophical speculation of the humanist, anti-humanist, posthumanist, and so on varieties—owes a debt to the work of Michel Henry, as we have seen, whose name appears overtly and covertly throughout Laruelle's work. In *Introduction to Marx*, Henry argues, contra Althusser, that the early *and* later work of Marx is squarely focused on the radical reality of embodied human life. Henry argues that the split between Marx's work and Marxism is that the former begins with the embodied, real, concrete existence of human life whereas the latter begins with the abstractions of "class," "history," "economics," and so forth. Henry acknowledges the innovative power of these abstractions for thinking through and resisting capitalism. But one errs, in Henry's judgment, if one loses sight of the embodied reality of human life. The abstractions of Marxist philosophy are grounded in "what radically opposes it," writes Henry, "the most radical and most particular determination – the individual."[14] Here it must be emphasized that by "individual," Henry does not mean "individual" as understood within the normative frame of bourgeois thought. Henry's "individual" is not the liberal "subject." Henry's "individual" is not "man." Marx's "rejection of the essence of man," writes Henry, "does not entail a dismissal of the individual *qua* real individual."[15] Henry resorts to a series of adjectives to flesh out his concept of the "real individual." The real individual is "the living individual in the first place" with "existing determination" that determines an individual *qua* individual.[16] The real individual is "the real, living determined individual."[17] An aporetic limit is signaled here: there is no way to speak or signify the "real individual" without situating it in a language that in some measure always already abstracts it. Henry's solution to this is to axiomatically determine his concept of the real individual as an embodied reality "given" as a "phenomenologically grounded" reduction.[18] The phenomenological "given" of the materiality of the human body is the philosophical and justificatory grounds for Henry's interpretation of Marx's work. Henry's position is that Marx's work consistently exposes the insufficiency of economic, political, and social frameworks for the effective critique of capitalism because these are abstractions. The "real" ground of critique must be grounded in what is real as "given"—the individual. But, the "analysis ... that solves the enigma" of capitalist abstraction and "clears away this mystification," notes Henry "is philosophy."[19] This is where Henry and Laruelle part ways.

Laruelle agrees with Henry that Marxism cannot be grounded in the abstractions of economy, society, politics, and so forth, but he goes one step further. Laruelle argues that *philosophy too* cannot sufficiently ground the critique of capitalism. Hence, for Laruelle, the "real individual" is *not a philosophical subject*, not even that body taken as "given" by phenomenology. "Real individuals," writes Laruelle "are uncountable, unspeakable, indisputable."[20] They are "ordinary" and the ordinary is their secret, their mystery, their "mystical" dimension. It is this dimension that cannot be accessed by the instruments of rationality. The finite individual is "transcendental" insofar as it transcends the schemas of infinite speculation. But this "transcendence" is immanent and finite. It is the finitude of the immanent individual that supercapitalism cannot think. It is a mystery—even a mysticism—for it. But for the real individual it is an entirely ordinary experience. Laruelle writes:

> The "transcendental" instance par excellence [of the individual] is not Being but absolute immanence ... Prior to any other definition, "transcendental" means a radical immanence ... This is the very definition of that which is only absolute, the absoluteness of the

finitude of the absolute ... This *real identity* is the mystical; it is the foundation or the essence of the individual existent. Ordinary man is a "mystical" living being.[21]

The mysticism of the individual is of the orders of the ordinary and the Real. It is the ordinariness of embodied life that appears as a mystery to supercapitalism for it lies beyond the reach of its intelligibility. On this score, the succession of attempts to decenter the human subject by contemporary philosophy reflects (and reproduces) the capitalist imperative to dispel this ordinary mysticism of the individual in the name of what can be conceptualized, counted, grounded, and quantified. The concept of the finite individual as the subject of an ordinary mysticism also reflects Laruelle's structuralist orientation. The structuralist dimension is here visible at two levels. At one level, Philosophical Decision is the invariant structure of thought of which philosophy is one model (or representation); at another level, the "finite individual" is the name for what invariably escapes the structure of Philosophical Decision. These two levels might be described as an antimony between structure (Philosophical Decision) and event (finite individual). Non-philosophy is the thinking of this dyadic structure via dualysis *qua* method that thinks the dyad without recourse to the philosophical ruses of synthesis or sublation. We thus have a purely formal definition of the finite individual, negatively postulated, as that which cannot be the subject of supercapitalist rationality or Philosophical Decision and which thus appears *from the capitalist perspective* as mystical.

Laruelle turns both the reality and the thought of the individual toward a non-dialectical horizon, or a *negative dialectical* horizon (*pace* Adorno). I now turn to an examination of this mode of thinking via a comparative reading of Adorno's project of negative dialectics and Laruelle's project of non-standard Marxism. Laruelle's structuralist presentation of Philosophical Decision and of the finite individual is affine with Adorno's "negative dialectics." Both modes of thought operate with the fused principle of non-equivalence/non-exchangeability of philosophical concepts and the Real. It is this principle that Adorno calls "nonidentity." Moreover, the tradition of thought for which Adorno stands—Critical Theory—is comparable to non-philosophy (and indeed to non-Marxism). For what Critical Theory elaborates is in fact a *critique of philosophical systems* and all instrumentalized rationalities that underwrite the continuance of (capitalist) domination or what Adorno calls "administered life."

Excursus on Exile and Style

Before embarking on a comparative reading of negative dialectics and non-philosophy, permit me to preface it with an excursus on exile and critical style. The experience and concept of exile is decisive for non-philosophy and negative dialectics. Adorno's exile, first in New York and later in California, was to profoundly impact his life and thought. It was in exile that he composed *Minima Moralia* and, with Max Horkheimer, *Dialectic of Enlightenment*. Adorno's fate as an exiled Jew was marked by consistent reminders that philosophically, politically, and professionally he was largely homeless. The experience of exile for Adorno was a conceptual and moral imperative that expressed itself in his interdisciplinary and transdisciplinary migrations across philosophy, sociology, politics, and art. As Adorno writes in *Minima Moralia*, "it is part of morality not to be at home in one's home."[22] Living rightly as an intellectual means not being at home or otherwise too comfortable in whatever national, cultural, intellectual, or political field one finds oneself in or passing through. The peripatetic nature of Adorno's intellectual, professional, and personal itinerary through geographical and conceptual locations—both by force and by choice—constellated itself into a moral and intellectual imperative to refuse the easy comforts of ideological and national belonging. Edward Said, the most important theorist of exile in the twentieth century, saw Adorno as an exemplary icon of what he called "metaphysical exile," which is that cultivated sense of intellectual "restlessness, movement, constantly being unsettled and unsettling others."[23] One can detect this trait of "metaphysical exile" across Adorno's philosophical corpus. His interventions range across disciplines in a critical, but not systematic way. The fragment, not the whole, is the organizing motif of his work.

Negative Dialectics and *Minima Moralia* are exilic exercises. They take the reader (as they did their author) through philosophical terrains that are not systematically bounded. The gaps between the fragments in each text are spaces for readerly travel and conceptual migration. The moral of each text as *Minima Moralia* declares, again, is "not to be at home in one's home." We are instructed as readers to always be prepared to go. The very style of Adorno's writing enacts an exilic practice of theory. Philosophical systems, for Adorno, are mere way-stations, or put otherwise, raw materials, for the construction of constellated concepts that illuminate an exilic itinerary. As Said puts it in *Representations of the Intellectual*:

The core of Adorno's representation of the intellectual as permanent exile, dodging both the old and the new with equal dexterity, is a writing style that is mannered and worked over in the extreme. It is fragmentary first of all, jerky, discontinuous; there is no plot or predetermined order to follow. It represents the intellectual's consciousness as unable to be at rest anywhere, constantly on guard against the blandishments of success, which, for the perversely inclined Adorno, means trying consciously *not* to be understood easily and immediately.[24]

Adorno's style of writing was inspired by the most difficult of modernist art forms—abstract painting, atonal music, and modernist theater—which refuse the capitalist imperative of easy consumption. Martin Jay rightly identifies Adorno's work as an attempt at "atonal philosophy" in the spirit of Arnold Schoenberg's atonal music.[25] Adorno's very way of writing expelled the harmonies, syntheses, and reconciliations of Hegelianism in favor of an abiding dissonance between concept and Real. "Schoenberg's revolution in music," writes Susan Buck-Morss "provided the inspiration for Adorno's efforts in philosophy … For just as Schoenberg had overthrown tonality, the decaying form of bourgeois music, so Adorno … attempted to overthrow idealism, the decaying form of bourgeois philosophy."[26]

To overthrow the decayed form of bourgeois philosophy, however, also involved a salvage operation of sorts. Above all, Adorno sought to preserve a *concept of the individual* from bourgeois philosophy albeit one remodeled on the principle of *nonidentity*. The individual, for Adorno, is that radically subjective form of experience consistently violated and objectified by administered life under capital. It is that idiosyncratic remainder that cannot be assimilated by the identity-logic of consumer-being. It is this remainder of subjective experience that modernist art at its best speaks to. Allow me to quote at length from Adorno's *Aesthetic Theory*:

> For the artwork and thus for its theory, subject and object are its own proper elements and they are dialectical in such a fashion that whatever the work is composed of – material, expression, and form – is always both. The materials are shaped by the hand from which the artwork received them; expression, objectivated in the work and objective in itself, enters a subjective impulse; form, if it is not to have a mechanical relationship to what is formed, must be produced subjectively according to the demands of the object. What confronts artists with the kind of objective impenetrability with which their material so often confronts them, an impenetrability analogous to the construction of the given in epistemology, is at the same time sedimented subject: it is expression, that which appears most subjective, but which is also objective in that it is what the artwork exhausts itself on and what it incorporates; finally, it is a subjective comportment in which objectivity leaves its imprint. But the reciprocity of subject and object in the work, which cannot be that of identity, maintains a precarious balance.[27]

The art and theory that Adorno supports are those forms of making and thinking that place subjective and objective domains into a dialectical reciprocity, but of a kind that "cannot be that of identity." Adorno's phrase—"cannot be that of identity"—is an imperative. What Adorno's form of theory cannot tolerate is the dialectics of identity. The modernist artwork is iconic in this respect for Adorno. The modernist artwork—for, example, the monochromes of Kazimir Malevich—is an icon of nonidentity between objective and subjective. Nonidentity is a state in which the poles of subject and object are placed into a dialectical relation but without synthesis or resolution. The material conditions for the production of the artwork that confronts the artist is "analogous to the construction of the given in epistemology" insofar as the raw materials for the making of art have to themselves be produced just as the "given" of philosophy is not actually given, but has instead to be produced. The differential chasm between the subjective experience of art and the objective historical and material conditions of its production cannot be reduced to a single moment or movement of identity. The two are caught in a constant to and fro that excludes the possibility of synthetic resolution. The confrontation with objective conditions of production (broadly conceived) dialectically forces to the fore the subjective dimension as precisely that dimension expelled by objective conditions of production. What is true of the modernist artwork for Adorno is true for his readers.

To read Adorno is to consistently find oneself unmoored, but in that unmooring the reader's exilic subjectivity manifests. Adorno's alien and inhospitable lines of text refuse any subjective luxuriation. But in that frustrated pleasure one discovers a subjectivity proper to the alien and inhospitable world of administered life. "Adorno's thesis," writes Robert Hullot-Kentor, "that subjectivity could only be transcended by way of subjectivity, and not by its limitation, is one way of formulating his seminal insight: that identity is the power of nonidentity."[28] Aesthetics at its best illuminates the experience of the identity of subjectivity in and through "the power of nonidentity," which is to say through the power of the negative. Theory and art must "use the strength of the subject," writes Adorno, "to break through the fallacy of constitutive subjectivity."[29] The subjectivity that breaks through the fraud of subjectivity is like that "finite individual" we encounter in Laruelle's work. It is that form of subjectivity that in its nonidentity and non-exchangeability enables a novel conceptualization of individual as ordinary mystery from the *point of view of supercapitalism*. The fallacy or fraud of "constitutive subjectivity" is the fraud of supercapitalist capture, namely, the fraud that holds that the individual can be traded for the capitalist concept of the individual *qua* consumer-producer.

It is the uneasy consumption of Adorno's prose that reveals a radically subjective dimension harboring within the objective (and objectified) conditions of commodification. Adorno reminds us in *Negative Dialectics*: "No theory today escapes the marketplace."[30] Theory cannot escape the marketplace, but this condition does not destroy the possibility that theory—like art—can still contain within it a resistant kernel that cannot be easily accommodated to objective conditions of marketization. Something inscrutable and idiosyncratic remains in Adorno's prose that makes that marketability difficult. His texts are openly antagonistic toward the imperative of ease and readerly comfort. Adorno's style, though strikingly original, is not expressive but muted and stifled into a paratactic staccato voided of humanist warmth. And "just opening to any page," writes Hullot-Kentor of *Aesthetic Theory*, "without bothering to read a single word, one sees that the book is visibly antagonistic. No one from the land of edutainment would compose these starkly unbeckoning sheer sides of type."[31] The reader is forced back on their heels unable to find any foothold on the cliff walls of sheer theory. But this very absence of a home in the text radically discloses a subjectivity that experiences its exile from the land of identity. I want to suggest that negative dialectics is affine with non-philosophy especially in its non-Marxist form. If non-philosophy is the non-domination of the Real by thought, then what must be prized and developed are those instances of nonidentity that scramble in advance the pseudo-domination of the Real by concepts.

Negative Dialectics

Negative dialectics is not in any sense a negation of dialectics. It is rather its radicalization. It radicalizes the insufficiency of concepts to what they conceptualize. For Adorno, dialectics is *in practice* a consistent demonstration of conceptual insufficiency. Adorno reads the Hegelian "absolute" as a posited name that identifies what dialectics *cannot but not achieve*. "The name of dialectics says no more," writes Adorno, "than that objects do not go into their concepts without leaving a remainder, that they come to contradict the traditional norm of adequacy."[32] Dialectics *in practice*, for Adorno, always brings thought into *contradiction* with the "traditional norm of adequacy." The traditional norm of philosophical adequacy fails in dialectical thinking, because dialectical thought inexorably leads itself by way of abstraction beyond the object it seeks to arrest. Adorno writes that "dialectics drives beyond every particular."[33] Dialectics is driven and motivated to overshoot the particular because its gaze is fastened on the whole even if that whole is only an illusion.

Negative dialectics radicalizes what *in practice* standard dialectics always shows: the insufficiency of concepts to capture the Real. "My thought," writes Adorno, "is driven to it [negative dialectics] by its own insufficiency."[34] This *insufficiency* is rooted in Adorno's axiom that every conceptualization of an object leaves a nonconceptualizable remainder. What Adorno calls "identity thinking" cannot tolerate this leeching of the Real beyond the concept. The closest standard philosophy comes to the nonconceptual (and the nonidentical with the concept) is what standard dialectics identifies as "contradiction." But contradiction is simply "nonidentity under the aspect of identity," notes Adorno.[35] Negative dialectics holds to the principle that the Real remains in some measure absolutely nonconceptualizable precisely because the Real is not merely conceptual. Negative dialectics begins with the part, the fragment, but not the part or fragment of some whole or absolute. Its aim is to arrest absolute particularity. This attempt always fails—the concept, general by nature, always overshoots or undershoots the particular—and precisely because of this the "negative" of negative dialectics is affirmed in the operative failure of its own conceptual work. We then have in negative dialectics an ethics as much as a philosophy.

Negative dialectics is to an extent a regulative idea—an ethical aspiration—more than a practicable mode of philosophizing. Negative dialectics as a method is committed to nonidentity thinking, but it self-consciously and self-critically knows that this in some measure is impossible. As Adorno admits, "identity is inherent in thought itself. To think is to identify."[36] Negative dialectics is the practice of an exilic self-estrangement from identity-thinking. But this exilic journey can never come to rest. It continually renews the migration by moving toward the horizon of the nonidentical and nonconceptual. "The matters of true philosophical interest," writes Adorno, "are those in which Hegel, agreeing with tradition, expressed his disinterest. They are nonconceptuality, individuality, and particularity."[37] Saving the finite, the individual (object and subject alike) means thinking so as to save the particularity of particulars by negatively indexing those nonconceptual remainders produced out of every dialectical maneuver.

Negative dialectics was born not only of Adorno's critique of idealism—and his radical concern for the finite and material particulars of artworks—but it was also born out of desire to philosophize according to the reality of the administered world of capitalist domination. Hegel's thought prized the absolute. Hegel's yearning was premised on a vision of a world in which thought (or spirit) develops freely and rationally. But for Adorno this is precisely what was false in Hegelianism. The modern world is *systematically unfree*. At the same time, Hegel's system perfectly suits an unfree material world. Hegelian dialectics reflects a world where particulars are made fungible by conceptualization. In "the administered world," writes Adorno, "the impoverishment of experience by dialectics ... proves appropriate to the abstract monotony of the world."[38] In other words, the impoverishment of particular and concrete experience at the hands of idealist dialectics drains the world of experience of all but what can be accommodated to (idealist) thought, but this is fitting in a world where everything that is not exchangeable (for a concept as much as for cash) goes unthought anyway. Thus, Adorno's work in *Negative Dialectics* is an attempt to place the non-exchangeability of the Real (or nonconceptual) at the center of thought without subordinating the Real (*pace* Laruelle) or the nonconceptual (*pace* Adorno) to thought itself.

It is important to note again that negative dialectics does not imagine that the concept can be disposed of and the nonconceptual grasped in its phenomenal purity. "Necessity compels philosophy to operate with concepts," writes Adorno, "but this necessity must not be turned into the virtue of their priority."[39] The priority accorded to the concept over the nonconceptual/Real must be deprioritized so that it does not rigidify into a reified virtue. At the same time, however, Adorno notes, "criticism at that virtue" should not "be turned into a summary verdict of philosophy."[40] In other words, there is no easy way out of identity-thinking. There is no getting around concepts in the field of thought. "In fact, no philosophy," writes Adorno, "not even extreme empiricism can drag in the *facta bruta* and present them like cases in anatomy or experiments in physics; no philosophy can paste the particulars into the text, as seductive paintings would hoodwink it into believing."[41] The question for Adorno is: how can one write in a way that self-reflexively understands theory's commodifiable condition while struggling assiduously against that condition and its affine constraints? The style of philosophical propositions is, for both Adorno and Laruelle, as important as their propositional content.

Disenchantment of the Concept

Negative Dialectics reflects Adorno's Weberian conviction that his own time was marked by the "disenchantment of the concept."

Whereas Max Weber famously defined modernity as the epoch of disenchantment—religious, magical, mythical disenchantment—Adorno was concerned with the disenchantment of philosophical reason. Just as it had once been possible to imagine a divinely ordered world, so the Enlightenment imagined a rationally ordered world subservient to the dominion of human reason. But this for Adorno was the myth that underwrote modern thought itself. Whereas before magical thinking had constrained the free exercise of reason, now reason itself had withered under the constraint of a world ordered by the identity-logic of capitalist exchange. The hoped-for "system" of modern reason is haunted through and through by the spirit of the system of economic exchange. The prizing of freedom by idealism negatively indexed the absence of that freedom—or the reality of "unfreedom" in Adorno's language—within society. "The system is not one of absolute spirit," writes Adorno, "it is one of the most conditioned spirit."[42] This "system" is "the subjective preconception of the [objective] material production process in society," which is always, dialectically speaking, "the unresolved part, the part unreconciled" with the subject.[43] The hoped-for state of absolute freedom, and the hope that this could be conceptualized by philosophy, could *only be hoped-for* because it is impossible to achieve this within a constitutively unfree *system*. The concept of system has a double meaning for Adorno. It refers at once to both the unfreedom of philosophical systems and the unfreedom of the societies that produced them.[44] Specifically, the rule of "identity" in standard dialectics is the philosophical symptom of the rule of identity or sameness that conditions the "system" of exchange value. Fredric Jameson writes that:

> Identity ... is in fact Adorno's word for the Marxian concept of exchange relationship (a term he also frequently uses): his achievement was then to have powerfully generalized, in richer detail than any other thinker of the Marxist or dialectical tradition, the resonance and implications of the doctrine of exchange value for the higher reaches of philosophy.[45]

Negative dialectics aims at thinking according to non-exchange value metrics in order to negatively redeem nonidentity *qua* the non-exchangeable and non-equivalent; to allow dialectics to be haunted by what it cannot think according to the logic of supercapitalism. To be clear: negative dialectics cannot think nonidentity positively. It can ascribe no positive content to this category. But it can think nonidentity as that which is impossible to conceptualize using identity-thinking (or standard philosophy). Negative dialectics is centered around an absent center—a negative center—which is precisely the negative of exchange value or *use value*. The method of negative dialectics itself negatively indexes what is missing in the social world, namely, the revolutionized conditions that would allow us to think according to use value, and to think this independent of its dialectical and diabolical double, exchange value.

Jameson's reading of Adorno's project in *Negative Dialectics* enables him to win Adorno for the Marxist cause for he shows how the logic of Adorno's position tracks closely to Marxian categories. "A passing remark early in *Negative Dialectics* makes it clear," writes Jameson, that "its themes are first and foremost to be grasped within another tradition" than idealist dialectics, "namely the Marxist" tradition. "This crucial passage," continues Jameson, "identifies 'what cannot be subsumed under identity' – that is to say everything that has been evoked variously under the notions of difference and heterogeneity, otherwise, the qualitative, the radically new, the corporeal—'as what is called in Marxian terminology, *use value*.'"[46] If "system" for Adorno means both economic system and system of ideas, then negative dialectics will have been that form of thought resistant to the enforced systematicity of both. I say "will have been" because, as Adorno makes clear, this resistance is always already undermined because negative dialectics is inscribed within the identity-logic of standard philosophy and the historical conditions of unfreedom that underwrite all philosophy in the time of capitalism.

Negative Dialectics and Non-Philosophy

Negative dialectics and non-philosophy are philosophical projects, but they are structured in non-standard forms. Both projects inscribe a certain impossibility into their logics. They are each interestingly self-defeating as they use concepts in a way that aims to disenchant conceptual production itself. Recall again Adorno's statement: "Necessity compels philosophy to operate with concepts but this necessity must not be turned into the virtue of their priority no more, than, conversely, criticism at that virtue can be turned into a summary verdict against philosophy."[47] A perfectly dialectical statement, Adorno here early in *Negative Dialectics* signals that no virtue of priority ought to be accorded thought nor should one thoughtlessly prioritize the critique of this virtue. I take this to be proximate to Laruelle's call not to abandon philosophy, but to defetishize its prioritization by treating it as material to be worked anew. "We could ask," writes Laruelle, "why should we ... deprive ourselves of the benefit of philosophy? In reality, we are in no way whatsoever deprived of its benefits. Philosophy still ... enters into it [non-philosophy] as an essential part of its materiality."[48]

To understand conceptual production as "material" is to understand it as something that can (and should) be workable. It means resisting the ideological conception of concepts as reified categories of understanding. It means being a maker and not only a thinker of thoughts, or, put differently, it means thinking thought as making and vice versa. Making thought, for Adorno and Laruelle, means making thought's insufficiency with respect to the Real thinkable. The gap between thought and Real is not another dualism in the classical Cartesian sense. The gap is inscribed in the Real itself. *We can only think the Real in reality by its immanent resistance to thought.* Freed from the spell of full epistemic access, philosophy returns as material to be worked in ways that hold the Real open, but decisive in the last instance even while this instance can never be an instance for philosophical thought. "Freed from philosophical sufficiency," writes Laruelle, "non-philosophy neither has to reduce ... nor to exclude the multiplicity of philosophies. On the contrary, it frees rhetoric in order to enrich and modify the philosophical material."[49] Philosophical materials can be treated then as what they really are: a set of tropes, figures, rhetorical strategies, which when freed from the structure of Philosophical Decision, empower a thinking otherwise than deciding and philosophically limiting the Real. We enter the indefinitely bounded space of signs *in* the Real and exit the *camera obscura* of philosophical capture and pseudo-objectivity.

Similarly, Adorno operates from within the enclave of philosophy in order to carry out a critique of the supercapitalist "system" immanent to philosophy and to the administered lifeworld under capitalism. *Negative Dialectics* is not a work in the *philosophy of Marxism*, but quite literally, a *Marxist critique of philosophy*. Philosophy is shown to be poisoned by the pill of exchange and equivalence such that to speak of a "philosophy of Marxism" would be, for Adorno, a bastardization. "Marxism" is a form of thinking (and writing) that resists the idealist trappings of philosophy by obliquely shifting philosophy's gaze in the direction of all that has historically and materially conditioned every standard philosophy). Adorno's and Laruelle's projects share elective affinities. Each operationalizes a critique of philosophy from *within philosophy* by treating philosophy as material shot through with the reminders and remainders of all that is unfree in any "system" of thought born of the social lifeworld of exchange. Here I follow Dave Messing who identifies Laruelle's project as a "critical" project affine with the critical project of Adorno inasmuch as both seek to challenge the hegemony of philosophical reason in the name of saving the nonconceptual (*pace* Adorno) or the Real (*pace* Laruelle).[50] I am admittedly forcing a parallel between the nonconceptual and the Real. But I hope that this forcing proves at least useful for thinking how each theorist opens the question of Marxism beyond standard philosophy by in effect demonstrating that "Marxism" might name precisely the limit of what can be thought against supercapitalism from within supercapitalism. What is gestured (sometimes inchoately) in the work of each theorist is an attempt to index a non-capitalist, non-exchanged-based, or simply non-supercapitalist mode of thought. I want to emphasize that neither Adorno nor Laruelle "exit" philosophy. Rather, they enter its domain by an oblique angle from which two perspectives in one become visible: the system of thought and the system of exchange. This is two perspectives presented as a "vision-in-One." Each project makes visible capital *in and as* standard philosophy. Philosophy and capitalism are not only analogous structures; they are determined by the same disavowed decision, namely, *thought-for-the-Real*. Adorno and Laruelle axiomatize the failure of exchange and equivalence in conceptual production in order to index not only what survives, but that which determines the possibility of thought itself—the Real (Laruelle) or the nonconceptual (Adorno). The resistance mounted by negative dialectics and non-philosophy alike is a structural resistance to the structure of "economy" that spans the "system" of philosophy and that of capitalism. But whereas the structural critique of philosophy links the projects of negative dialectics and that of non-philosophy, the latter diverges from the former inasmuch as Laruelle speculatively recasts Marxism in explicitly *impossible* terms.

Impossibilization

Laruelle asks: "what is to be done with Marxism?"[51] What is to be done with this wealth of raw material crafted first by Marx, under conditions of destitute poverty, in the name of all who suffer in poverty and destitution? What can this discourse do, or what can be done to it, in order to continue to resist today what Marx resisted in his time? How do we continue to wage war on the logic of abstract value and against all the exterminationist imperatives and impulses immanent to the reproduction of capitalist normalcy? To impossibilize Marxism means rewriting (by cloning) it in a form that is conceptually inoperative for the purposes of deciding the Real. Non-Marxism will have been—for it is an ongoing process—that mode of theory by which Marxism is made to continually struggle against the very philosophy within which it is captured. Non-Marxism will have been the cloned *syntax of the Real* in a world ruled by abstraction. Ethically it will have been radically committed to sundering the philosophical couplet of *thought-for-Real* in the name of the radically Real.

Laruelle's non-Marxist work consists of a set of *introductory* gestures in *Introduction to Non-Marxism*. I insist on the conceptual relevance of the first word of the title inasmuch as the text importantly and significantly is an "introduction," not only to a way of rethinking Marxism in non-standard ways, but also for the very processes by which Marxism and the "non" of non-philosophy may be "superposed." The word "introduction" fittingly signals a provisionality that functions as an auto-critique of presumptive mastery. The text refuses to be yet another final word on what Marxism must be or become. Rather, it radically renders the final word "impossible" by dismantling the operative mechanisms that would make non-Marxism immediately applicable as a recipe for freedom from the reign of unfreedom in "free market" societies. In this respect, it is affine with the tradition of Adornian critique for it negatively indexes the conditions of unfreedom that disallow the easy implementation of a *socialist economy of thought*. This is precisely why Laruelle begins with the discourse of "failure" in the Marxian heritage. The "failure" of Marxism is radically recast by Laruelle as that which "fails" to conform to the imperatives of exchange and equivalence. The socialist demand is always a demand for the "impossible" from the perspective of capital. That may seem quite obvious. But the theoretical implications are profound.

The impossible socialist demand is theoretically rendered by Laruelle as an ethico-politico-theoretical stratagem of impossibilization. One must here exercise due caution in reading Laruelle on Marxian impossibilization. It could quite easily default into an impoverished "Derridean" reading of a socialism "to come." That would have the unfortunate effect of making the socialist demand into a kind of regulative idea that would remain always over the horizon theoretically and practically speaking. Impossibilization is a *theoretical procedure* that aims to "introduce" the concept of impossibility into the matrix of theoretical Marxism and thereby face the political legacy of the socialist failure in a move that neither minimizes nor reifies the challenges of that history. "Situations of defeat or retreat, as much as those of victory," writes Laruelle, "are the worst situations that the rigor of thought has to confront."[52] The victories and defeats—both ethically and politically—that have transpired under the sign of "Marxism" have created exceptional difficulties. It has symptomatically surfaced in the long history of repeated "returns" to Marx or turns to historical precedents prior to Marx. It has surfaced in accusations and counter-accusations of "deviations" and "heresies." It has surfaced in the insistent search for some purer form of Marxism and the result is that the Left has been tragically fragmented and internally divided by the very weapons it sought to use against capital.

The question of the "failure" of Marxism "should not be left to what occupies the 'post-Marxist intellectuals,'" writes Laruelle, who are merely "monetizing some revamped ideas still useful to today's tastes."[53] Nor is the question to be given over "to philosophy alone or to science alone, not even to their combination, meaning we shouldn't leave it to Marxism itself."[54] Marxism itself is a history of the fragmentation of its profile into political and philosophical stances and struggles. Is then the failure that of philosophy or of practice or still of their "scientific" combination? Laruelle writes:

> These failures are heterogenous and incommensurable, their doctrinal "set" is nothing less than what will be its form of "totalization" or theoretical organization. Looking at this explication of the multiple aspects – *as such* – of failure, an explication that is not empiricist concerning one of them or though one of them alone, we postulate that the theoretical genre of Marxism is a new type, unknown within philosophy … but which still rightly forms itself here under the dominant drive of philosophy.[55]

The "failures" of Marxism—or what is presented as failures under the sign of "Marxism"—are heterogenous. These diverse failures require diverse analyses. But the popular judgment from the Right and sometimes from the Left is that the failure of Marxism is global and total. But a "totalizing" judgment of this sort is to be expected "under the dominant drive of philosophy." Again, if philosophy, as Laruelle defines it, is the judgment or decision on the Real, then a philosophical judgment on Marxism will be "totalizing." And this is precisely what we see. The diverse problems of Marxism are treated as a unitary problem and judged as a failure to realize the Real philosophically. This philosophical judgment itself fails to recognize the diverse political and philosophical investments and struggles that go by the name of "Marxism." It reifies "Marxism" as a unitary sign with a unitary signified. Laruelle writes:

> A non-philosophical repetition of Marxism cannot therefore be motivated ... by its effective or "historical" failure, with the unilateral interpretations that accompany it. We have no criteria with which to affirm its reality, and what type of reality it is. In general this conclusion is arrived at specularly, moving from a specific failure to a global failure. For example, from the collapse of historical and political communism to the local or even general collapse of theoretical Marxism. This is a confusion of genres, it suffers from a thousand nuances or precautions already made by others. Therefore there is an imperative rule: a theory of Marxism's failure cannot itself be Marxist ... Or to put it another way: Marxist theory cannot be a duplication of history, but a duplication with a "difference" (nearly a "contradiction") without risking the return to the specular merry-go-round of philosophy.[56]

The failure of specular, or speculative (i.e., "philosophical"), Marxism, for Laruelle, stems from a confusion of the "genres" of Marxism. It confuses Marxism's practical history with Marxist theory. To fuse these genres into a globalized judgment is to be expected when philosophy is the dominant drive of Marxism. Laruelle's corrective is to follow Marx's theoretical form. Marx constructed his theory out of history in order to represent it with a revolutionary difference. "Marxist theory cannot be a duplication of history, but a duplication with a difference." This means only that Marxist theory, in the non-philosophical register, must be politically and theoretically faithful to

Marx's method, which is to think historically without confusing the historical record for the Real of Marxism in the last instance. Marx examined the historical development of industrial capitalism in order to identify in its failures the potentialities for a revolutionary surpassal of its historical conditions. Likewise, the failures of the Marxist political project should be examined in order to find in those very failures the symptomatic trace of philosophical decisionism that judged Marxism a failure. Marxism has always already failed according to the dictates of supercapitalist ideology. But, Laruelle notes, it "remains to be determined as real within its being-impossible."[57]

It is possible (and easy) to determine Marxism to be a failure or impossible by simply delivering it "to the 'digestion' of history."[58] But, for Laruelle, no narrative reconstruction of the "history of Marxism" suffices or substitutes for Marxist theory. To reduce Marxist theory to the history of Marxism—which would be to reduce history itself to historicism—is a lazy means to ratify a totalizing philosophical judgment on Marxism in the guise of *merely doing history*. Laruelle's intervention on this point is decisive and his statement deserves careful attention. Laruelle writes:

> It is one thing for Marxist theory to be "impossible" from the point of view of the World and history. But it remains to be determined as real within its being-impossible so as not to deliver it to the "digestion" of history, to its dissolution within capitalism, neither making its historical failure eternal, rendering it definitive through some transformation that we would impose upon it. This passage from a capitalist impossible to a real impossible takes the form of non-Marxism.[59]

History we have been told for decades has reached it terminus and capitalism has shown Marxism to be a failure. But the political defeat of Marxism should not be confused with a determination that Marxism as such is impossible. The Philosophical Decision regarding the supposed failure of Marxism works by a sleight-of-hand whereby Marxism is traded for its political history. The "non-Marxist kernel" of Marxism remains to be "possiblized" within the historical verdict that declares it impossible.[60] The impossibility of reducing Marxism *qua* theory to Marxism *qua* history reveals its radical kernel. It is the gap between these two levels that Laruelle seizes upon. For Laruelle, the problem is to radicalize this impossibility by severing Marxism both from its historicist and theoreticist reductions. The "kernel" that remains is, however, not a "rational" kernel that need only be "released from Marxism, but which in the end must be transformed."[61] Thus, Marxism must be repeated by the introduction of the "non" into its theoretical materials through a non-philosophical mode of articulation set against historicism and *all* forms of decisionist thought. "*Only a ... non-Marxist repetition of Marxism*," writes Laruelle, "can avoid the ideological comedy of the philosophical 'return' as the tragi-comedy of its deconstruction."[62]

Marxism from the supercapitalist viewpoint is impossible. And it seems impossible from the historicist viewpoint as well. So much for our capitalist world and our inherited historicist ideologies. But Laruelle argues that Marxism "remains to be determined as real within its being-impossible." What could this mean? Something of Marxism "remains" that cannot be reduced to the supercapitalist judgment. We might formulate this radical remainder as: *Marxism should be impossible to conceptualize as anything but a failure from the capitalist and historicist worldviews.* Marxism is that "subject" which is impossible to accommodate to *philosophical* logic. Marxism is that impossible *stranger* in history and in the prison-house of capitalism; it is that "negative" moment (*pace* Adorno) that haunts the easy positivism of capitalist and historicist thought. And it is the resistant remainder that non-Marxism seeks to develop. But how? By what forms and procedures can this impossibilization be realized? Laruelle's answer: "fiction." The question inscribed in that answer is the subject of the next chapter.

5

Fiction

What must non-Marxism be if it is not to default into a supercapitalist form? Laruelle's answer: *fiction* or *philo-fiction* to be exact. This chapter situates the concept of philo-fiction via a comparative reading of Laruelle and Jean Baudrillard. The conceptual stratum underlying their differing (though not irreconcilable) concepts of fiction is what I hazard to call "non-dialectics." I argue that the form of non-Marxist fiction must be non-dialectical in the last instance. To fictionalize Marxism in non-dialectical terms amounts to a way of thinking that repudiates the logic of exchange and equivalence in order to think against capital in non-capitalist terms. Finally, I examine what the significance of Laruelle's theory of Marxian fiction is *qua* theory via an examination of his structural use of quantum tropes.[1]

Dialectics

Fredric Jameson argues in *Valences of the Dialectics* that the term "dialectics" historically had two distinct, but interrelated, meanings. "Traditional presentations have tended to stage the dialectic either as a system on the one hand, or as a method on the other," writes Jameson, "a division that faintly recalls the shift from Hegel to Marx."[2] Jameson argues that both these presentations have grown increasingly untenable in the contemporary period. The idea (or ideal) of philosophical systematicity has been dethroned. Marxist dialectics—dialectic as method—has also been beset by debate and division over the question of the correct application of the dialectical method to history. Whether taken as method or as system, however, dialectical philosophy is an attempt to temporalize philosophical concepts: to think in time. A properly dialectical concept is self-reflexively defined by the contradictory conditions that establish the possibility of its own conceptualization. Dialectics repudiates the idea that there are timeless concepts that make reality thinkable. Reality itself is a historically contingent (if not determined) concept for the dialectician. Indeed, as Jameson shows, the argument over whether dialectics is a method or a philosophy presupposes a thoroughly "undialectical" conception of method and philosophy.[3]

However, if one does not in some way lend the concept of dialectics "structure" then there is no way to define dialectics apart from its own conceptual history. One is then faced with the problem of the tension—perhaps dialectical tension—between structure and event.

Dialectically speaking, there cannot be in principle something called "the dialectic" as that would uncritically presume a mode of thought that is singular and not subject to history. But if there is no such thing as "the dialectic" as such, then there is only a series of historically competing dialectical methods. But dialectical method implicitly presumes some structural invariance. "Examples are the arbitrary cases that rattle around inside the impossible abstraction called a law," writes Jameson, and this "law" of the same that would identify examples of dialectical thought as truly dialectical would be but the displaced name for "the concrete universal."[4] For Jameson, pluralizing and temporalizing the concept of the dialectic does not allow us to escape the binding claim of universality that conditions the possibility of the concept of "the dialectic" as the foundation stone of all dialectical philosophies and methods.

Internal to the method/philosophy debate concerning dialectics, however, is a presumption that dialectics is somehow suitable to the thinking of history. Either it is presented as the privileged method for distilling the meaning of history or it is presented as the ontological foundation of history itself. Either way dialectics as an idea is taken to be sufficient to its assigned task to capture the Real of history. Baudrillard and Laruelle strategically and critically intervene precisely on this question of the dialectical capture of the Real. Their non-dialectical modes of fictionalized theory turn on the problem of the Real itself. It is to this that we now turn before returning later in the chapter to the matter of dialectics and finally fiction.

The Real

I want to briefly but concretely review the status of the Real in both Laruelle and in Baudrillard as it is crucial to my argument. In *Principles of Non-Philosophy*, Laruelle spells out his axiom of the Real. The Real is nothing less than the radicality of immanence prior to any concept or Philosophical Decision on the Real. The Real is that which is always already the prior condition for the possibility of philosophy and all its decisions. Laruelle writes:

> Immanence of the Real ... without a single morsel of transcendence (of the World, language, movement, topology, set theory, etc.) – of philosophy. It is what it names ... an *autonomy through radicality* in relation to every form of transcendence. Phenomenally, it is a "Given-without givenness."[5]

Laruelle's prose is complex. But his point is relatively simple. The Real is not a philosophical concept. The Real transcends philosophical reason but only by virtue of its immanence. As Ian James notes in *The New French Philosophy*:

> [T]he real is transcendental ... insofar as it is *its own* condition. The real does not need anything other than itself and its own indivisibility in order to be what it is: this is its absolute autonomy and self-sufficiency. Yet the real is real (a lived, "unreflective" experience), it is also the condition of all being, existence, thought, consciousness, transcendence, and so on since all these are (in) the real, or put differently, the real is always immanent to them.[6]

James precisely captures Laruelle's concept of the Real as self-sufficient and autonomous. Yet this apparently transcendental abstraction—the Real—is entirely immanent and lived. Put simply, the Real does not stand outside the Real. Philosophy is "in" the Real and determined by it in the last instance. Laruelle insists on the phrase "in-the-last-instance" in any formulation concerning the Real. It functions as a means to signal that the Real is determinative of thought while simultaneously signaling that there is no means to spell out that determination without reproducing the logic of Philosophical Decision. The concept of "in-the-last-instance" performatively resigns the authority of "standard philosophy" to decide the Real. Non-philosophy takes this resignation of authority as a point of departure for reworking philosophical concepts—via strategies of fictionalization—in order to *think through philosophy* without presuming to know or decide what is decisive—the Real.

The objects of non-philosophy consist, as already noted, of what Laruelle calls "clones," which look like standard concepts, but are used in non-decisionist ways. Laruelle assembles these clones into fictional texts or "philo-fictions." Fiction should be understood here in Laruelle's special sense. Laruelle explains in *Philosophy and Non-Philosophy* that philo-fictions have two "surfaces." "On one of their surfaces, they [philo-fictions] will be *scientific representations*," writes Laruelle, "that utilize philosophical elements," which is to say philo-fictions represent a certain open-minded, experimental approach to the raw materials of philosophy, but "on the other surface, they will be philosophical fictions, fictions 'for' philosophy."[7] "Non-philosophy must use philosophical language as its material," writes O'Maoilearca, but it does so by "transforming its syntax ... [b]y cloning philosophical statements shorn of their transcendental ambition."[8] By this operation of philosophical denuding, non-philosophy transforms philosophical materials so as to make them *radically transcendental*, entirely estranged from their decisionist mandate.

Philo-fictions experiment with the raw materials of philosophy precisely by *taking them as raw materials* rather than as elements of a systematic set of coordinated decisions on the Real. This experimental or "scientific" approach yields a fictionalization of philosophical systems. Philo-fiction occupies a parallel space to that of standard philosophy. As Anthony Paul Smith notes "the purpose of [Laruelle's] fiction is a kind of counter-creation to the world."[9] By refusing to legitimize the gesture of philosophical decisionism, philo-fiction constitutes an auto-critique of philosophy's *a priori* assumption that it is sufficient to philosophically know and determine the Real. "The act of creating fiction is the goal of non-philosophy," writes Smith, "in order to relativize and disempower what presents itself as sufficient and absolute," namely philosophy itself.[10] Philosophy auto-valorizes itself through the establishment of a sovereign discourse on/over the Real. In materialist philosophies—including many strains of Marxism—this presumption is reflected in propositions regarding the *materiality of the material world*. But Laruelle rejects this too even while he remains ethically and politically committed to the stated political investments of the Marxist materialist tradition. But he rejects any claims on the "world" *reflected* in philosophy's mirror. This is why Laruelle consistently capitalizes the word "World," because, like the Real, it is a transcendental signified invented and operationalized by philosophical reason. Laruelle's critique of the concept of "world" is affine with others of his generation, especially Badiou.

Philosophical concepts of "world" tend to function as alibis for pragmatism and reformism. "Be practical!" "Get real!" "This is the real world." These are colloquial versions of a philosophy of subjugation that prizes reconciliation with a hollow and hopeless concept of the "world." But the world operative in such instances is not the Real according to Badiou. For him, the Real is what can always be punctured and broken in two by the "event." Thus, Badiou polemically and critically refuses what Peter Hallward calls philosophy's "worldly condition."[11] Badiou refuses to accommodate his thought to a concept of world that refuses to recognize its potential for radical eventual ruptures. "Badiou's philosophy," writes Hallward, "is infused with that same contempt for worldliness characteristic of the great antiphilosophers, most obviously Saint Paul and Pascal. The world, as such, is defined for Badiou by imperatives of communication and interest."[12] This concept of the world (or World in Laruelle's language) is an alibi for conformist thought that disavows eventual possibility.

However, despite a degree of convergence between Laruelle's and Badiou's critique of the concept of "world," their projects are in detail entirely opposed. Badiou (unlike Laruelle) remains committed to concepts like Being and Truth whereas Laruelle suspends these concepts—in a kind of radicalization of the Husserlian *epoché*— in order to treat philosophical texts as raw material for thinking otherwise than that demanded by the decisionist imperative of standard philosophy. Laruelle's inventive and creative skill at disempowering and defetishizing philosophy comes to the fore in his book-length critique of Badiou: *Anti-Badiou: On the Introduction of Maoism into Philosophy*. There Laruelle clones Badiou's concepts in order to produce at times a parodic fictionalization of Badiou's philosophy. Laruelle challenges what he sees as the authoritarian dimension of Badiou's thought. Laruelle zeroes in on Badiou's well-known axiom that *mathematics equals ontology*. Badiou "manages to divest us of all our predicates and reduce us," writes Laruelle "to the state of a proletariat at the service of a mathematico-philosophical dictatorship."[13] But Laruelle insists that the non-philosophical task should not be to critically deconstruct Badiou's system for to do so would re-aggrandize the philosophical stakes of Badiou's thought. Laruelle writes that his aim is:

> not a dialogue, it is ... an ultimatum, but emitted ... from an acknowledged position of weakness, in an encounter with a position of acknowledged force [i.e., Badiou's position] ... An ultimatum signifies that we are not the mirror of the other. Very precisely, Badiou is a means for non-philosophy ... Thus, this book is, above all, finally ... a book in which non-philosophy explains itself to itself, but with the aid of a counter-model that it falls to us to transform.[14]

Laruelle's text on Badiou is a model of *fictionalized* theory. Laruelle takes Badiou's "system" and voids it of its imperatives and decisionist valances. The terms of Badiou's system are rewoven, reworked, and reproduced into a fictionalized "clone" of the system. The critique of Badiou's system via fictional strategies of parody, exaggeration, and juxtaposition constructs a counter-theory that calls for the "liberation" of theory from philosophical claims on the Real and indicates a path forward for theory that properly de-reifies standard philosophy's stature while enabling the continuance of emancipatory thought on the plane of theory itself. For Laruelle, the best part of Badiou is his positioning of philosophy as materially determined by knowledge practices external to it in the fields of love, science, art, and politics. But what he objects to is that these modes of knowledge production ultimately serve as philosophy's material whereas philosophy is subject to nothing and therefore technically sovereign and autonomous. Laruelle's fictionalization of Badiou strategically operates between parody and critique. Badiou is also an occasion for

Laruelle to consider the philosophical stakes of the "anti" position notable in philosophy from Marx and Engels to Badiou himself. Allow me to quote Laruelle at length:

> [T]he present book ... attacks a philosophical personality recognized as very significant. It is thus indeed an Anti-Badiou, and critiques "a" philosophy through an individual in perfect concord with it. But Anti-Badiou prepares only a non-philosophy, and certainly not an anti-philosophy. The point that may attract most attention is not the main objective – which is, more broadly, a dismantling of the facilities, procedures, and paradoxes of *every* philosophy, through the treatment of one particularly brilliant example. The rules of the "anti-" genre are not firmly established: there is the critique, the polemic even, but this is not a specifically philosophical genre – its ... always a little *ad hominem*. And non-philosophy is precisely, if one might say so, *ad hominos* – it is an act of defense ... the defense of a certain human universality against an individual spokesperson of a tradition that is believed to place it in danger.[15]

Let us pause here. What is decisive in these opening pages is Laruelle's move to at once position his theoretical efforts as an *ad-hominem* attack against Badiou as a figure of a certain philosophy—what he calls elsewhere *philosophy in person*—but he also here positions non-philosophy on the side of the "defense of a certain human universality" against the authoritarian and annihilatory logic not only of Badiou's philosophy but of *"every"* philosophy. Here Laruelle appears to be cloning Marx's attack in *Poverty of Philosophy* and *Theses on Feuerbach*. In the former, Marx attacks the rule of economic reason via the figure of Proudhon, and in the latter, he attacks so-called materialist philosophy via the figure of Feuerbach. Both are attacks on philosophy and on the embodiment of *philosophy in person* in defense of a "certain human universality." Marx's texts like Laruelle's *Anti-Badiou* straddle polemic and critique in such a way that is not properly (or solely) philosophical. The "anti-" genre is strategically deployed by both Marx and Laruelle in order to at once critique a certain philosophy and *every philosophy* in the name of what resists every Philosophical Decision. Laruelle continues:

> It is important to mock the adversary, to make him ridiculous given the opportunity, and one thereby achieves various all-too-easy effects. If Badiou is really a "great philosopher," he bears overly apparent traces of it. The contrast between the academic master and the stellar celebrity, the mandarin and the emperor, produces a comical effect ... [In] his militant [posture], his posture of mastery, his intellectual becoming, his obsession with greatness ... it is difficult not to see oneself, faced with this Goliath, in the position of David – difficult not to imagine one of those antique philosopher clichés, crushingly dignified, impeccably trained, draped like those statues sculpted in eternity that Nietzsche evokes ... and whose theatre Heidegger tried to rebuild for us. He wears all the signs of greatness ... [with] his grandiloquent and grandiose interventions, his masterful poise, his authoritarian style, ... his way of making a statue of his stature. But the lampoon, as inevitable as it may be, is a poor weapon here ... The adversary must be taken seriously, treated as exceptional.[16]

It is "important to mock the adversary" in the "anti-" genre (as Marx does especially in *Poverty of Philosophy*) precisely to bring the "greatness" of a philosophy (and a philosopher's) stature—the stature of a great statue—down to earth. But to bring *philosophy in person* down to earth can also itself fall prey to a "grandiose" philosophical imaginary by imagining the critic in the guise of David slaying Goliath. This theater of combat (David and Goliath) or iconoclasm (statues) is "all-too-easy" to fall prey to in the case of a philosopher like Badiou whose ego is legendary and whose mediatized stature is that of a "great philosopher" of militancy and the event. But while parodic "lampooning" is a necessary instance of the genre of "anti-" critique, it too readily risks the reestablishment of the "grandiose" terms of philosophical "greatness" by transferring them into the terms of the great critique. Thus, lampooning must give way to a gesture that accords the enemy a seriousness that comedic parody implicitly contains but which is masked by its own irony. Serious critique and ironic lampooning are superposed here in order to ventriloquize the materiality of Badiouan philosophy for the purposes of an experiment in non-philosophical thought. In this way, Laruelle makes of Badiou's philosophy a means "by which non-philosophy explains itself to itself."[17]

Laruelle's fictionalization rebels against the authority and authoritarianism of Badiou's philosophy and through it *every* philosophy. This fictionalization should be understood in its most radical sense. The fiction that interests Laruelle is not constrained by any theory or philosophy of fiction nor by any conceptual apparatus that would decide in advance its epistemic status. As O' Maoilearca astutely observes:

> If the Real is ... "nothing but real," then fiction ... must no longer belong to the "order of the false." ... And such a reconfiguration of fiction requires a rebellion against "philosophy's authority" over it: fiction must no longer be subordinated to the judgements of philosophy. Instead philosophy will be made to "reenter" through fiction and be conceived as a mode of fabulation ... an avowedly *utopian* form of thought.[18]

One cannot "apply" non-philosophy any more than one can "apply" fiction. Rather, one *non-philosophizes philosophy* in the name of liberating thought from its standard addiction to dominate and decide the Real. The aim of this liberation is to repurpose philosophemes (voided of their decisionist character) within a fictional ensemble that maps out a theoretically utopic position liberated from the closed dialectic of the Real. It is here that Laruelle's position intersects with Baudrillard's to which we now turn.

Baudrillard's concept of the Real is by no means identical to that of Laruelle's. But his axiomatic starting point yields a similar mode of utopic theorizing that he calls "theory-fiction." As is well known, the central axiom that organizes Baudrillard's best known work is that of *the disappearance of the Real*. "On the horizon of simulation," writes Baudrillard, "not only has the world [or the real] disappeared but the very question of its existence can no longer be posed."[19] It is this disappearance that "defines the irresolvable relationship between thought and reality," notes Baudrillard, inasmuch as "a certain form of thought is bound to the real."[20] That "certain form of thought" is none other than that of dialectics. Dialectical theory, continues Baudrillard, "starts out from the hypothesis that ideas have referents and that there is a possible ideation of reality. A comforting polarity, which is that of tailor-made dialectical and philosophical solutions."[21] Opposing dialectical thought—thought that presumes a critical interface with a preexistent concept of the Real—Baudrillard advocates for the writing of "theory-fiction." As Baudrillard notes in an interview:

> My way of reflecting on things is not dialectic. Rather, its provocative, reversible, it's a way of raising things up to their Nth power, rather than a way of dialectizing them. It's a way of following through the extremes to see what happens. It's a bit like theory-fiction.[22]

Baudrillard never really spells out exactly the form fictionalized theory is supposed to take for good reason. Theory-fiction is not a systematic theory, but a process of invention that "challenges" the theoretical privilege accorded the Real. One might say that theory-fiction represents what Laruelle calls "non-analysis," which deflates and defetishizes the typical subjects of critical theory: power, domination, political economy. His search for a theoretical topos of thought unencumbered by a concern for the Real marks the late Baudrillard as a thinker of utopia *in theory*. As Mike Gane notes, Baudrillard's later work evinces an "undeniable vitality and creativity coupled with undying fidelity not to a utopian vision in the passive sense, but to a passionate utopian practice in theory."[23] This use of fictional strategies to force open utopic spaces in theory is a trait shared by Baudrillard's "theory-fiction" and Laruelle's "philo-fiction."

In 1972 with the publication of *For a Critique of the Political Economy of the Sign*, Baudrillard sought to augment and critique bourgeois *and* Marxian political economy alike. Baudrillard argues that both traditions erred by theorizing a restricted economy or closed conceptual system in which production, exploitation, and consumption cycle predictably through the matrix of "use value" and "exchange value." Baudrillard argues that under late capital, exchange value is complexified by the exchange and circulation of signs. Baudrillard takes the art auction as an example of this. Wealthy people buy blue-chip art at the auction not merely to purchase art, but also to show that they have the financial power to do so. Here, as Baudrillard acknowledges, he is building on the work of the late-nineteenth-century economist Thorstein Veblen.

In *Theory of the Leisure Class*, Veblen argued that the principal form of labor performed by the "leisure" class consists of social acts of "conspicuous consumption." The "process of *consumption* considered as a *system of sign exchange value*," writes Baudrillard, is "not consumption as traditional political economy defines it ... but consumption considered as the conversion of economic exchange value into sign exchange value."[24] Bidding at the art auction, again for example, is not simply an economic transaction; it is a system of sign exchange through which bidders exchange social signs of wealth and leisure. Baudrillard contextualizes his project in *For a Critique* as part of an "exiled" and marginalized tradition of political economy. As he notes:

> Critical theorists of the political economy of the sign are rare. They are exiled, buried under Marxists ... Veblen [is] the great precursor[r] of a cultural analysis of class, which beyond the "dialectical materialism" of productive forces, examines *the logic of*

sumptuary values which assures and perpetuates through its code the hegemony of the dominant class.[25]

It is the process of sign production that traditional political economy does not account for and thus cannot resist. A critical theory of consumer society must then begin by integrating the analysis of sign exchange "into the very structures of political economy."[26] But as Baudrillard notes this is strongly resisted by bourgeois and Marxian theorists alike. He writes:

> [T]he traditional boundaries of political economy, canonized by bourgeois economic science and Marxist analysis should be disregarded. And the resistances to this are strong, for they are of all the orders: political, theoretical, phantasmagorical. Yet today only a generalized political economy can define a revolutionary theory and practice.[27]

Bourgeois and Marxian political economy alike traditionally rely on restricted models of economic production. But the meaning or value of a sign is open, contingent, and mutable. Baudrillard thus challenges both traditional semiotic theory (Saussure), since he rejects the anchoring force of the "signified" as a metaphysical mechanism designed to restrict the contingent economy of meaning; and he rejects Marx's anchoring concept of "use-value" as incompatible with the social labor of conspicuous consumption. *For a Critique* articulates a "*generalized political economy*" in Georges Bataille's sense of "general economy." In *The Accursed Share*, Bataille famously distinguished between "general" and "restricted" economies. The former names economies in which some expenditure remains expended and does not return in another form; whereas the latter names economic systems, like capitalism, that are *philosophically premised* on the Philosophical Decision that everything is exchangeable for its equivalence in another form. Baudrillard's *form of critique* is in this sense a *general economy in theory* inasmuch as it is organized around "general principles" of sign exchange that cannot be anchored in the Real of classical exchange nor in the transcendental signified of classical semiotics.

By the late 1970s, Baudrillard and Laruelle come to see that the problem is how to escape the auto-valorizing force of dialectical philosophy and to open *anew the problem of the politics of theoretical critique itself*. Neither thinker seeks to overthrow or overcome dialectics for that would simply reaffirm dialectics itself. Rather, each invented strategies of theoretical writing that intensify the potential for emancipatory thought immanent to the ethics of Marxism without getting ensnared in the dialectic of exchange (or the rhetoric of production as we will see). This project is affine to an extent with Jean-François Lyotard's *post-Marxist* work of the same decade. Lyotard's *Libidinal Economy* of 1974 sought to tap into and exploit what he called the "intensities lodged in theoretical signs."[28] However, in the same text Lyotard surprisingly rebukes Baudrillard. A brief detour through Lyotard's critique of Baudrillard suffices to spell out the difference between the fictionalized Marxism of Baudrillard and Laruelle and the libidinalized writing of Lyotard's post-Marxism. That difference, as we will see, is the difference between a *theoretical indifference to the Real* (Baudrillard and Laruelle) and the continuation of dialectics in a new way (Lyotard).

Lyotard's Objection

Lyotard's major statement of post-Marxism is *Libidinal Economy*. The text stems from the tradition of Freudo-Marxism, albeit in a highly creative and "literary" style that challenges that tradition. Lyotard argues that Marxian political economy is torn between two warring poles, which he names, somewhat regrettably, the "prosecutor Marx" and the "little girl Marx." Lyotard reads Marx as trying to engineer a theory to close and contain industrial society's "erotic" fascination with the object (capital) that he was trying to theoretically prosecute. Lyotard's corrective is to explode political economy via a libidinalized textualism. Lyotard writes:

> we are not going to do a critique of Marx, we are not, that is to say, going to produce the theory of his theory; which is just to remain within the theoretical. No, one must show what intensities are lodged in theoretical signs, what affects within theoretical discourse; we must steal his affects from him. Its force is not at all in the power of its discourse, not even in inverse proportion to it, this would still be a little too dialectical an arrangement.[29]

For Lyotard, theory is now to become a kind of literary art form. He goes on to explicitly target Baudrillard's work for ultimately not pushing his own "theory-fiction" far enough and for what he sees as Baudrillard's racialized and imperialist valorization of the prelapsarian economics of "symbolic exchange" before the Real disappeared into the play of signs. Lyotard writes:

> How is that [Baudrillard] does not see that the whole problematic of ... symbolic exchange ... belongs in its entirety to Western racism and imperialism – that it is still ethnology's good savage, slightly libidinalized, which he inherits with the concept?[30]

Lyotard argues that his libidinal approach to theoretical writing evades the traps of dialectical Marxism and the imperialistic fantasies of Baudrillard's alternative by entirely exiting the discourse of standard political economy via a libidinalized mode of writing that aims not to diagnose, but to actualize "intensities lodged in theory," or what Geoff Bennington interestingly calls, "writing the event."[31] Lyotard's writing aims not to theorize capital, but to write the dissolution of political economy (and theory broadly) and to actualize this event of dissolution through what might be called the *jouissance of the signifiers of theory*. Lyotard seeks to "demonstrate that the cold serious discourse of political theory," writes Bennington "is also a set-up of libidinal economy."[32] And, as noted, Lyotard damns Baudrillard's concept of "symbolic exchange" as nothing more than an alibi for the lost contact with a concept of the Real. Baudrillard's figure of "symbolic exchange" is read by Lyotard as the symptomatic sign that Baudrillard cannot relinquish his own desire for the Real if only as a lost sign or lost time. Baudrillard remains wedded to the paradigm of political theory dialectically hinged on the (lost) Real prior to capital. Baudrillard in short is still too much concerned with the Real and with the critique of capital than his prose admits.

However, one could say nearly the same of Lyotard. His desire to escape theory via a libidinalized textual free-play is itself a dialectical gesture. In working through the tensions between theoretical analysis and an inscriptive desire to exceed analytic limits, Lyotard reproduces dialectics as he shuttles between what one is tempted to call a prosecutorial Freudo-Marxism and a polymorphous and perversely polysemic excess of writing. Without this background tension, the book would hardly have the charge it does. It is precisely because Lyotard is working against the backdrop of Marxism and psychoanalysis that he can make the apparent dissolution of these theories an exciting literary event. *Libidinal Economy* is squarely situated within the dialectics of theory and practice: *the practice of theorizing the end of theory.*

Theory-Fiction

Contra Lyotard, I want to suggest that the surpassal of dialectics lies not in the direction of a libidinalized writing, but in a form of thought *axiomatically structured by a radical indifference to the Real*. Baudrillard's indifference to the Real—which became far more pronounced in his later "theory-fictions"—was, however, nascently emergent in *For a Critique*. That work is organized around the thesis that a culture of sign-exchange is symptomatic of the loss of contact with the Real. Baudrillard further radicalizes his theoretical indifference to the Real in his landmark statement of post-Marxism: *The Mirror of Production*. There Baudrillard singles out the Marxist concept of "production." He argues that the concept of "production" morphed into a "strange contagion" in post-1960s Left theorizing.[33] Baudrillard detects symptoms of this "strange contagion" in everything from the "unlimited 'textual productivity' of *Tel Quel*, to

Gilles Deleuze and Félix Guattari's factory-machine productivity of the unconscious," to Lyotard's libidinalized writing; "no revolution," it seem, Baudrillard writes, "can place itself under any other sign."[34] Baudrillard traces the theoretical valorization of production back to Marx himself. Baudrillard continues:

> Marx did not subject the form of production to a radical analysis any more than he did the form of representation. These are the two great unanalyzed forms of the imaginary of political economy that imposed their limits on him. The discourse of production and the discourse of representation are the mirror by which the system of political economy comes to be reflected in the imaginary and reproduced there as the determinant instance.[35]

Marx's decision on the nature of "man" as "productive animal" was never submitted to a radical analysis, according to Baudrillard. As Gane notes, Baudrillard argues that "Marx never gets to the position where he can challenge the thesis that the human is characterized by the capacity to produce."[36] Marx's concept of the human as productive animal was adopted from classical political economy as truth and this, argues Baudrillard, determined *and* limited Marx's thought. "What is necessary … is to see that a generic definition of man as productive animal, *homo faber*," writes Gane, "is actually caught within the effects of [the] rationality of capital itself."[37] Production, and its human correlate of labor power, constitute a closed circuit of philosophical decisionism that reproduces the image of the human *qua* producer in the mirror of bourgeois and Marxian political economy alike. Baudrillard reads Marx (but more Marxism) as having established a set of concepts—use-value, exchange-value, commodity-fetishism, and so forth—whose analytic value is pegged to a concept of the Real given under the sign of "production" and therefore ultimately subordinate to the logic of capital itself.

Marxism, according to Baudrillard, did not escape the *dialectical economy of knowledge qua production* organized by the theses and assumptions of classical political economy. "Marxism was not the revolutionary breakthrough that had been hoped for," writes Gane, "but catastrophically it was a particular elaboration of capitalism's own principles."[38] The system of political economy "rooted in the identification of the individual with labor power," argues Baudrillard, is naturalized in the theoretical mirror of classical political economy.[39] "Between the theory [of capitalism] and the object [of capitalism]," writes Baudrillard, "there is in effect, a dialectical relation, in the bad sense: they are locked in a speculative dead end" (29). Baudrillard concludes that production "must be submitted to a radical critique as an *ideological* concept."[40] This is a clear shot across the bow of Althusserian theory. Althusser's theoretical project was aimed at saving Marx's "science of history" by philosophically distinguishing "science" from humanist (and Marxist) ideology. So, for Baudrillard to claim that the "science of history"—the science of the history of modes of production—is an *ideological* concept inherited from classical political economy is to say that Althusserian Marxism remains ensnared in the self-imposed ideological limits of supercapitalist rationality. "The analysis, in Althusser, of theory as a productive process," writes Baudrillard, is "modeled on capitalist processes, and, as a system of thought, only reduplicates its object as separated and alienated: theory and revolutionary practice are neutralized by this failure."[41]

Mirror marks a break in Baudrillard's trajectory. There he breaks not only with Marxist productivism, but with a *theoretical mode of production* that produces the Real in its "mirror" of critical reflection. This is what links his "provocations," as Douglas Kellner calls them, with respect to Marx and Foucault. Two years after *Mirror*, Baudrillard published his "broadside attack, *Forget Foucault*," writes Kellner "at a time when Foucault was becoming a major figure in the pantheon of French theory."[42] Kellner continues:

> In many ways, *Forget Foucault* marks a turning point and point of no return in Baudrillard's theoretical trajectory. In this text he turned away from his previous apotheosis of a politics of the symbolic, and moved into a more nihilistic, cynical and apolitical theoretical field.[43]

It is true that Baudrillard's later work does not directly engage political questions. But what it does do is inventively and critically engage *the politics of theoretical critique itself*. This is the essence of *Forget Foucault*: it is an indictment of the valorization of power by Foucault and of desire by Deleuze and Lyotard. "Foucault," "Deleuze," and "Lyotard," for Baudrillard, name patterns of theory—*philosophies in person*—which reify the desire of power and the power of desire. This, Baudrillard argues, is theoretically complicit with the values of consumer capital. In *Forget Foucault*, Baudrillard writes:

> This compulsion towards liquidity, flow, and an accelerated circulation of what is psychic, sexual, or pertaining to the body is the exact replica of the force which rules market value: capital must circulate; gravity and any fixed point must disappear; the chain of

investments and reinvestments must never stop; value must radiate endlessly and in every direction.[44]

Baudrillard damns the libidinal turn in theory as a reflection and reification of what might be called in Deleuzian-speak the *desiring machine of capital itself.*

The question for Baudrillard post-*Mirror* becomes: how to escape the "spiral" of critical theory whose models turn into alibis for the domination of bodies, desire, and libido by consumer society? What can theory do? In what form might anti-capitalist theory continue? Fiction is Baudrillard's answer. In a brief essay titled "Why Theory?" Baudrillard writes:

> To be the reflection of the real, or to enter into a relation of critical negativity with the real, cannot be theory's goal … What good is theory? If the world is hardly compatible with the concept of the real which we impose upon it, the function of theory is certainly not to reconcile, but on the contrary, to seduce, to wrest things from their condition, to force them into an over-existence which is incompatible with the real.[45]

Strategies of fiction—such as exaggeration (forced over-existence), seduction, the wresting of things from their conditions—are *aesthetic solutions* to the problem of theory's relation to the Real in the age of its disappearance. It is no longer "enough for theory to describe and analyze," notes Baudrillard, "it must itself be an event in the universe it describes."[46] Theory-fiction, however, is not a mode of theory that ratifies defeatism as Baudrillard's critics often suggest. Theory-fiction can still "challenge" the economic, the social, the political, and the aesthetic. But as Baudrillard notes:

Even if it speaks of surpassing the economic, theory itself cannot be an economy of discourse. To speak of excess and sacrifice, it must become excessive and sacrificial. It must become simulation if it speaks about simulation, and deploy the same strategy as its object … If it no longer aspires to a discourse of truth, theory must assume the form of a world from which truth has withdrawn.[47]

The method described above may be fruitfully compared to Laruelle's strategy of cloning philosophy. Theory-fiction will sound like standard philosophy, but function more like literature. Just as literature creates a world (and that creation is an event in the world) so too does theory-fiction create a world with the capacity to think in ways unbounded by the constraints immanent to any pre-given concept of the Real. Baudrillard's post-Marxist theory-fiction, styled in a self-consciously avant-gardist manner, strategically offers a means to reanimate utopian thought. Theory "must tear itself from all referents," writes Baudrillard, "and take pride only in the future."[48] Baudrillard's theoretical posture post *Mirror* is to regard the Real with the same indifference that the Real regards theory. Here too Baudrillard's project theoretically intersects with Laruelle's.

Philo-Fiction

Non-Marxism is a fictionalization of Marx and the Marxist heritage. Its style is not so much the avant-gardist style of late Baudrillard as the cold and anti-humanist rationality of the early Althusser. But whereas Althusser sought to save Marx's science of history via philosophy, Laruelle seeks a "scientific" examination of standard philosophy. Laruelle's sense of "science" is attitudinal. It is an attitude open to experimenting with the raw materials of a philosophical text or tradition. "Rescuing Marxism from metaphysics is effectively an illusion," writes Laruelle, "as long as it is not rescued from philosophical sufficiency itself, belief in the Real, and desire for the Real."[49] This is the first meaning of "fiction" for Laruelle: escape from belief in, and desire for, the Real. Laruelle defines his approach to writing non-philosophical fiction thus:

> To under-practice philosophical language, indeed to under-understand it ... is to think in a more generic manner without exceptions. All this can appear too moral, but this would be forgetting that thought is not uniquely subtractive, it is [an] insurrection.[50]

The passage performs what it describes. It renders philosophical language in a style that subtracts the value of immediate understanding for an "under-understanding." What is at issue here (and in the "generic" practice of non-philosophy) is to disrupt the standard philosophical economy whose master formula is: *thought-for-the-Real*. Non-philosophical fiction aims to take philosophy out of dialectical circulation with the Real. This subtractive gesture ethically refuses to participate in the reification of the principles of exchange and equivalence that regulate standard philosophy or *thought-as-capital*. For, as Galloway notes, "exchange is not simply *a* philosophical paradigm for Laruelle, but *the* philosophical paradigm. There is no philosophy that is not too a philosophy of exchange."[51] Standard philosophy, insofar as it presupposes an operative principle of equivalence and exchange with the Real, according to Laruelle, is formally identical to the logic of capital. Laruelle's fiction attempts to break the couplet between theory and the Real. "No synthetic portmanteau, but non-localizable indeterminations in the philosophical sense," writes Laruelle, "a language brought to its simplest status and sufficiently disrupted in order for the superior form of expression certain of itself in the concept to be rendered impossible."[52] Philo-fiction disrupts the syntax and operativity of standard philosophical prose to render the equivalence and exchange principles (or the capitalist principle) of standard philosophy inoperative. Laruelle continues:

> Philo-fiction is a gushing ... and subtractive usage of the means of thinking, of philosophemes-without-philosophy, of mathemes-without-mathematics, and from here, all of the dimensions of philosophy [are] rid of their proper all-encompassing finality, an insurrection against the all-too great superior finalities.[53]

Laruelle's fictional approach to Marxian theory uses insurrectionary language—an insurrection within and against philosophy—operated on the immanent terrain of thought. "There is, for Laruelle, a way of valorizing fiction," writes Smith, "as a force of insurrection that disempowers the world and operates without concern for its parameters."[54]

Excursus on the Introduction to *Introduction to Non-Marxism*

Althusser was right to note the conceptual import of a theoretical text's "order of exposition." The order—the syntax—as much as the words themselves is often key to the ultimate import of theoretical statements. This reading protocol is also advisable when reading Laruelle's work. The very ordering of the terms and propositions of *Introduction to Non-Marxism* is materially decisive.

I would like to examine closely the opening lines of the text. "With the supposed failure of Marxism the question 'as a Marxist, or even a communist, what is to be done?' has taken on a new dimension: 'What is to be done with Marxism itself?'"[55] The phrase "as a Marxist or even a communist" placed in quotes identifies this phrase as the part of the text of "failure"—the legacy of 1989—and its philosophical apologists who have either sought a novel post-Marxism or have solidified their cultural capital by mediatized spectacles of repentance. The whole "coming of age" of many of the generation of 1968 is the spectacular form of this philosophical narrative in which the young finally come to their senses. These media intellectuals have reposed Lenin's question—what is to be done?—by turning it on Marxism. Laruelle clones this trope in order to open a "new dimension" within the narrative of post-Marxism.

The "failure" of Marxism as a narrative was philosophically instantiated, notes Laruelle, in "[s]ituations of defeat or retreat ... as much as those of victory."[56] And those who begin from the standpoint of remembered victories still too often pose the question of the future of Marxism "as a Marxist or even a communist," which philosophically incorporates and affirms the narratological imperatives of the story of "Marxist or even communist" failure. The question—"what is to be done with Marxism?"—is posed by Laruelle without ratifying either the narrative of failure as embodied in those who still identify as "Marxist or even communist" nor to "what occupies the 'post-Marxist' intellectuals, that is monetizing some revamped ideas still useful to today's tastes."[57] The "failure of Marxism" is an instance of Philosophical Decision in the classical form of the *empirical-transcendental doublet*. The empirical event of 1989 is transcendentalized and determined universally. And the various "returns to Marx" by "Marxist and even communist" intellectuals are precisely determined according to the same form. The empirical "text" of Marx or of communism is transcendentalized and universalized to establish the philosophical conditions of Marxian futurity. The non-philosophical project rejects both philosophical solutions and determines its response to the question—"what is to be done with Marxism?"—according to a "new dimension" that is the dimension of struggle immanent to the conditions of posing this question philosophically. Non-Marxism struggles against the philosophical struggle to determine the question—"what is to be done with Marxism?"—and that struggle itself constitutes "a non-Marxist practice of Marxism," which is "destined to struggle against the 'particular interests' of philosophical systems desperately trying to capture it."[58] These opening lines identify a common form—the capitalist-philosophical form—that underwrites the narrative of Marxian failure. The struggle introduced (if not codified) by the introduction to *Introduction to Non-Marxism* is to establish the meta-theoretical conditions for formalizing the matrix for a non-philosophical practice of Marxism.

Matrix of Fiction

Laruelle's disempowerment of the philosophy-Real dialectic radically defetishizes philosophy and devalues the whole schema by which the

Real is reified and reproduced in the cultural capital of philosophical critique. Laruelle's theorization of non-Marxist fiction is advanced as of late in the language of mathematics and quantum physics. Laruelle's use of the quantum concept of "superposition"—which names the non-locality of atomic interactions—has received a good deal of attention. But his use of the concept of "matrix" has not received its due. It is to the fictionalized use of this term that I now turn.

The concept "matrix" comes from the field of mathematics. A matrix is simply a rectangular array of data (numbers, symbols, etc.) arranged into rows. Matrices have many applications not only in mathematics, but also in engineering and physics. Indeed, the physicist Werner Heisenberg developed "matrix mechanics" in order to mathematize the probabilistic nature of quantum interactions. Laruelle's concept of matrix is cloned from mathematics and quantum physics, but it is reframed and redeployed in a fictionalized manner or through what he calls *art-thought*. Laruelle writes:

> The matrix is, in a way, the third term or the term index that assures the aleatory but necessary conjugation of the two instances, without imposing on them an absolutely necessary analytic or dogmatic link. It is a link, however, that will be as rigorous as possible without forming a closed system, but at best a theory or scenario of art-thought.[59]

The matrix, for Laruelle, is a theoretical apparatus for the combination of at least two instances of thought. The structuralist bent here is clearly evident, even though in the same text Laruelle notes that the model he proposes "is not structuralist but generic and quantic."[60] Laruelle evidently wants to distance his method from the structuralist lineage presumably because that school of thought historically faltered in its attempt to render the human sciences scientific and instead became an alibi (and a precursor) for an increase in their philosophical profile and status. Yet, it is hard to deny that a structuralist orientation clearly plays some role in Laruelle's work, which, as previously noted, has been detected by others.

The global claim that philosophy—all philosophy—is marked by an invariant structure of decision on the Real is a structural reading of philosophy. Laruelle's latent structuralism is also evident in his use of the language of combination, function, matrix, and especially that or invariance. Claude Lévi-Strauss, the father of structuralist anthropology, puts the matter succinctly: "the structuralist approach … is the quest for the invariant, or the invariant element among superficial differences."[61] I am less interested in prosecuting or defending the structuralist approach (whether in anthropology, non-philosophy, or elsewhere) than in calling attention to the attempt to construct an invariant logic out of heterogeneous elements using a matrix. Lévi-Strauss himself worked by deconstructing myths into matrices of operators. The method roughly proceeded in the following way: operators were recorded on separate cards and arranged into rows and columns to form a matrix in order to discover the rules that structure logical permutations within the account. In "The Structural Study of Myth," Lévi-Strauss devotes considerable space to discussion of the technical and logistical difficulties involved in constructing usable matrices.

> It should be emphasized that the task of analyzing mythological literature … and of breaking it down into its constituent parts

requires teamwork and secretarial help. A variant of average length takes several hundred cards to be properly analyzed. To discover a suitable pattern of rows and columns for those cards, special devices are needed, consisting of vertical boards about two meters long ... to compare the invariants.[62]

I find Lévi-Strauss's discussion of the difficulties of constructing his theoretical apparatus interesting for the way in which it calls attention to its material base (cards and boards) and a division of labor (researchers and "secretarial" help). It can be compared to a passage in Laruelle's *Photo-Fiction* where he assembles a device or "apparatus" for doing "art-thought."

Photo-fiction in fact designates the effect of a very special apparatus that one must imagine because it is not available in any store, being more theoretical than technological ... It must be capable of "photographing" (if we can still use this term with a number of quotation marks since it is a discursive photography rather than visual) ... How is this new "box," which we are going to call the "matrix," constructed on the model of the empirical apparatus? ... Here its internal operations are no longer materially or physically optical but intellectually optical. This apparatus produces a fusion as superposition.[63]

Laruelle "constructs" a non-physical theoretical "matrix" for the "superposition" (a term we will return to) of photography and philosophical aesthetics. Whereas Lévi-Strauss calls attention to the material basis of matrix-theory, Laruelle calls attention to its *purely conceptual character*. We could place the two—Laruelle and

Lévi-Strauss—as allegorical figures of two modes of structural thinking into a matrix in order to discover the invariance that binds the material and intellectual aspects of matrix-theory. But I will simply note here that the two rest on an invariant conception of theory as a mode of production for which a set of raw materials and "apparatuses" is necessary for that mode of production. But Laruelle departs from the matrixing procedure of standard structuralism (*pace* Lévi-Strauss) in his refusal to accommodate the philosophical conceit of essential structures.

There are no privileged starting points or inputs that can be deemed anymore essential than any others and therefore the potential for a theoretically infinite variety of possible matrixial fictions remains open in non-philosophy. "The matrix of fiction," writes Laruelle, "requires at least two variables in order to break down the appearance of unity [and] of unitary determinism."[64] Here the clone of "superposition" is decisive. An atomic state of superposition is not a unity of positions, nor is it determined absolutely (but only statistically). For Laruelle, "superposition" names a way of thinking fusion without synthesis and without determinism (except by that of the Real in the last instance). Laruelle advocates for a superposition of states of Marxist theory in order to follow what he sees as the radically democratic character of Marx's theory. What is needed is to rid Marxism of the endless accusations of heresies and deviations, its constant returns to the purity of Marxism, its tired orthodoxies. And while "structuralist" might fittingly name non-philosophy's judgment of the decisionist invariant that traverses standard philosophical practice, Laruelle also opposes any structuralist decision on the nature of Marxism.

"Every operation of structural Marxism," writes Laruelle, "takes place under the concealed authority of philosophy and contravenes Marx's *democratically theoretical* project."[65]

For Laruelle, Marx opened a field of thinking that demonstrated that any possible field of investigation can yield insights into the radical reality of capitalist domination. "Marx set about on the 'interlacing' ... of philosophical declarations, of historico-social analyses, and of propositions for political action," writes Laruelle, meaning that his work constitutes "an ontology of difference."[66] The plurality of contexts and the manifold fields of investigation that Marx politically worked within and intellectually pursued constitute an *ontology of difference in theory* that lends his work its *theoretically democratic* character. Marx's work "superposes" diverse intellectual strands into a unity that standard philosophers have never stopped trying to render as a *philosophically unity*. "The multiplicity of the 'sources' of Marxism," writes Laruelle, "is symptomatic of ... [the] 'baroque' character of this kind of theory... which philosophers hesitate before."[67] Marxism is a theory at once baroque and unified. There are many states and locations in Marxist theory and practice. Marxism is a unified, but not a totalized theory inasmuch as all instances are determined in the last instance by the radicality of the Real.

Non-Marxism then names a *theoretical democracy*. The language of mathematics and quantum physics operationalizes a mode of thinking that metaphorically enables us to think according to superpositions rather than exclusions. Let us provisionally call this fictional aesthetic a *quantum structuralization of philosophy*. Laruelle notes in his essay "Marx and Plank":

We introduce the quantum and, more generally, quantum theory into Marxism under the form of their superposition. With what effects? Globally, it is a matter of extending or broadening its critical and theoretical scope, of reinforcing its scientific rigor against its philosophical hesitations but also of decreasing its level of dogmatism, simplification, and violence … Precisely it is by submitting Marxism to the imaginary yet complex operation of quantum algebra, by proposing a Marxism-fiction, that we will have done with the bad philosophical imaginary.[68]

Quantum language is an operator—a matrixial input—that is superposed with Marxism in order to create a "Marxism-fiction." This fiction is designed to do away with "the bad philosophical imaginary" and to reopen Marxist science to experimentation on the terrain of the theoretical imaginary by producing models of thinking that in their very form are capable of instituting and defending Marx's theoretically democratic project. Here again we can detect a structuralist strain in Laruelle's thought. Marxism is identified by a singular invariant: it is a theory of how to imagine justice without relying on the exclusionary violence of philosophical decisionism.

Matrixing Laruelle and Baudrillard

Laruelle and Baudrillard deploy the concept of fiction always with a strategically placed hyphen: philo-fiction (Laruelle) and theory-fiction (Baudrillard). This gap between the terms in each pairing is crucial and can be best understood according to Laruelle's matrixial logic. The matrix, for Laruelle, names a dyadic assembly of terms and concepts—even their superposition—but not their fusion or synthesis. Kolozova grasps this precisely. In a Laruellean sense, "a dyad is radical insofar as its components are not determined by the relation of one of the elements to the other," notes Kolozova, "but rather by the real, inside the dyad itself ... In other words, the relation between the two is unilateral."[69]

The matrix names the conceptual space where the differences between the matrixed elements are preserved without sublation under the determining aspect of the Real. Matrix theory, in Laruelle's sense, is radically dyadic but not dualistic and "without unification or a dialectical outcome."[70] There is no dialectic to be imagined in matrixial terms between theory and fiction. But rather there is a deployment of their relation as a *relation of non-relationality* determined as such only by the Real in the last instance. But that instance is never an instance *for philosophy*. The hyphen is the matrix itself that holds both terms in a unilateral relation under the horizon of the Real. Fictionalized theory, in this sense, works by means of operators that enable one to solve problems in *theory*: they furnish tools to construct *mytho-logical* solutions to problems in dialectical Marxism. As Lévi-Strauss taught, myths firstly are a means to solve problems. For him, it was a structural invariant of all myths that they are *logical* because they make problems logical and thus solvable or at least rationally thinkable. Baudrillardian terms such as "gravity," "mass," and "nebulae" and Laruellean terms such as "superposition," "quantum," "algebra," and "matrix" organize a structure of thought designed to address questions concerning the science of Marxism.

Only a fool (and there is more than one out there) would take such language at face value.

Neither Baudrillard nor Laruelle makes any scientific statements regarding particle physics or cosmology. They use words to work out ways of thinking. The "look," the "image," the "simulacrum" of science in their fictionalization of Marxian categories operationalize a plurality of modes of thinking that are rightly attentive to potentialities inherent in theorizing as a means not to speak truth to power, but to empower modes that refuse the *philosophical* dichotomies of truth and fiction. Their fictive terms remain in a state of "impossible exchange" (*pace* Baudrillard) that conceptually resists the invariant principles of exchange and equivalence that underwrite capitalism and philosophy. It resists the *philosophical pretension* "whereby the real submits to the true," writes Kolozova, "rather than the other way around."[71]

The matrix of "fiction" also constitutes a means for "dualysis"— Laruelle's "scientific" method—by which dualities of non-relationalities are preserved via modes of thinking and writing—that mimics or "clones" the way the Real "contains" phenomena without unifying them according to any number of philosophical variants of the doctrine of monism. "By way of 'dualysis,' the non-philosophical posture of thought and language mediates its object of knowledge," writes Kolozova, "while submitting to the *diktat* of the real. It establishes *mimesis* of the posture of scientific thought … while operating … [on] philosophical material."[72] Fiction is a mimesis or clone "of the posture of scientific thought" which treats materials—philosophical, transcendental, metaphysical, political, and so on—in a way that is attentive to their differences without submitting this schema to the *purely philosophical organization of a "philosophy of difference,"* but rather organizes a matrix of differences and non-relationalities that clone the unilaterality of the Real. This quasi-structuralist mode of matrixial theory given under the signs of "philo-fiction" (Laruelle) or "theory-fiction" (Baudrillard) make possible ways of thinking Marxism as the name for creative ripostes to the domination of thought and life in the name of all that is human and all that is humane in the last instance.

6

Metaphysics

The aim of this chapter is to elucidate what I call the *Kolozovan variant*. Katerina Kolozova is faithful to the spirit of non-Marxism (and non-philosophy generally), and she is one of Laruelle's most critical and inventive readers. But she has also developed a unique variant of non-Marxism oriented toward a reframing of critical animal studies, feminist, and gender theory. This chapter focuses on Kolozova's development of non-Marxist metaphysics. Integral to her radical conception of metaphysics are "physicality," "language as automaton," "instances of the real," the "dyadic self," and "formalization." These concepts are marshaled into a formidable arsenal for the critique of capital. The chapter concludes with an overview of Kolozova's anti-sacrificial economy of politics and finally with an explication of her radical metaphysics.

Physicality

The first thesis of the Kolozovan variant is that the thought of Marx is not materialist, but *physical* in the last instance. Marx, of course, was clearly influenced and shaped by his acute understanding of the long history of materialist philosophy. His doctoral dissertation for the University of Jena examined the difference between the materialism of Epicurus and that of Democritus. And, of course, Marx is popularly associated with "materialism," "historical materialism," and "dialectical materialism." But Kolozova argues that Marx's relationship to the *philosophy of materialism* is largely critical and at times openly hostile. On Kolozova's reading, Marx brought materialism down to earth. Marx, she argues, rejects traditional questions of philosophical materialism: the ultimate nature of reality, the problem of free-will, consciousness, and other assorted philosophical chestnuts. Marx was concerned with the material conditions that make life livable. Kolozova seizes on Marx's language of "human sensuousness" and "reality" in order to mount a non-standard materialist account of Marx and Marxism faithful to the logic of physicality and the radicality of the Real in the last instance.

Kolozova argues that Marx's theoretical work was marked by the consistent search for an exit from contemplative materialism. We see this clearly, again, in his attack on Feuerbach. Marx asserts that Feuerbach's materialism is only *contemplative*. The order of concepts in the opening lines of *Theses on Feuerbach* is decisive. "The chief defect of all hitherto existing materialism – that of Feuerbach included – is that the object, reality, what we apprehend through our senses, sensuousness, is understood only in the form of the *object of contemplation*; but not as *sensuous human activity*."[1] Note that Marx first cites the "chief defect" of "all hitherto existing materialism." Marx's critique is *firstly* a critique of *all* existing materialist philosophies. The "chief defect" of "all hitherto existing materialism" is that its "object" is "conceived only in the form of the object of contemplation." The "chief defect" is that materialism is conceptual: it exists only as a philosophy in the form of an object of contemplation. The problem is that the object of materialist contemplation—that of "reality" and "human sensuous activity"—eludes contemplation precisely because practical "reality" is not firstly contemplative, but real, physical, actual.

Kolozova seizes on Marx's invocation of "sensuousness" and formally clones it as: *physicality as instance of the real*. Wherever "one would expect ... the term 'materialism' or the material to appear in a writing by Marx," writes Kolozova, "regardless of whether [it is] the young Marx or the mature Marx, 'the real,' 'the sensuous,' and 'the physical' are used instead."[2] Kolozova's reading is amply supported by Marx's *1844 Manuscripts*. There, as we have seen, Marx theorizes "estrangement" as the estrangement from one's physical body as well as one's work. Labor exhausts the body. But this feeling of exhaustion is not even one's own since it is paid to capital in exchange for wages. Physical feeling—"sensuous human activity"—is estranged by unfree labor. The worker's feelings are not her own since she does not own her embodied means of production. Marx argues that the physical capacities of the laborer's body are used up as they are rendered and converted into objects (i.e., commodities) in a process he calls the "objectification of labor." The objects of estranged labor, commodities, stand opposed to the *physical subject* of the worker and in the process the latter cedes economic and political power to the former, which is to say that workers find their own physical constitution subjugated by the commodities that they produce. But Marx adds that the estrangement is two-sided: not only is the worker estranged from the products of labor, but also from laboring itself. Marx writes:

In both respects, therefore, the worker becomes a servant of his [sic] object, first, in that he receives an *object of labor*, i.e., in that he receives *work*; and secondly, in that he receives means *of subsistence*. This enables him to exist, first, as a worker; and, second, as a physical subject.[3]

Estranged labor is that condition whereby one owns neither the product nor the process of production. One "receives" work by "taking a job" that one pays for (and I include cognitive work here) by physical exertion. The perversity of capital is that it creates the subject position "worker"—which ontologically speaking is a secondary position relative to the fundamental primacy of one's existence as physical subject—but this existentially secondary position is made primary under capital. One is forced first to work to physically survive. For Kolozova, *critical resistance* proceeds via a *non-philosophical work on philosophical raw materials* that begins with the axiomatization of the primacy of physicality, not materiality, which is a philosophical concept. Kolozova argues that Marx's critique of capital and philosophy are part and parcel of one and the same effort to think from the perspective of the physical. Capitalism and philosophy share the same hatred for physicality. Both seek to annihilate concrete physicality and valorize abstract value. Kolozova writes:

> Following Laruelle, I argue that philosophy is constituted in a fashion perfectly analogous to the one which grounds capitalism – philosophy constitutes a reality in its own right and a reality that establishes an amphibology with the real (acts in its stead, posturing as "more real than the real"). In the split of the physical from the real of sensations of pain and pleasure, the detached body and mind

meet in order to produce "material" effects – an instance which we shall call "the real," … which constitutes estrangement as oppression, a characteristic of both philosophy and capitalism.[4]

But estrangement is not simply the enemy to be overcome by non-Marxism. As Kolozova suggests, the pain or pleasure of estrangement is an index of what cannot be assimilated by any philosophical or economic logic, namely, the Real or what Kolozova calls an "instance of the real." Estrangement in this optic is a radically resistant remainder and reminder of that which is real and thus escapes the epistemic capture of abstraction and linguistic signification.

Language as Automaton

Kolozova deploys the term "language as automaton" to mark those processes immanent to language that produce signification. "The category 'automaton' as used here," writes Kolozova, "does not refer to machines as automata but rather to the signifying automaton or language as automaton."[5] The "automaton of language" functions in diverse ways that are significant for Kolozova's analysis. These include the "value exchange system of capital, language as in natural languages," writes Kolozova, "but also in computer program languages, and, finally patriarchy as the exchange of phallic power by way of the currency/fetish of the woman and the feminine."[6] The structural invariant that links these phenomena is that each operates as instances of exchange: money for goods (capital), words for things (natural languages), commands for operations (computer languages), woman/feminine for phallic power (patriarchy). These "languages" function as automatons. These systems are driven by the immanent logic of exchange and equivalence and the valorization of value. These systems are also teleologically oriented toward the annihilation of physicality: women under patriarchy are objects of use and exchange, signifiers are ghostly traces of absent presences, capital converts physical reality into "pure" value.[7]

Kolozova draws an important lesson from Marx's famed formula of capital: M-C-M (Money-Commodity-Money), which reduces finally to M-M' (Money-Money prime). Commodities are only a relay—and a form that can be expunged—in the repetitive valorization process. Kolozova draws from this a stinging indictment of the annihilatory logic of capitalist patriarchy. "Just as the 'C' in the M-C-M formula can be expunged," writes Kolozova, "so, to paraphrase Marx, because not an atom of matter enters the composition of woman as commodity, the material woman can be excluded from the equation P(hallus)-P(hallus). The less physicality in the pure value of femininity the more perfect the finite automaton of patriarchy."[8] The "perfect" automaton of patriarchy—like that of capital—is achieved by the annihilation of physicality via the production and valorization of value. Capital's devaluation of the physical—whether of the body, labor, articulation, and so on—parallels the valorization of "thought" in philosophy. Philosophy (like capital) is a "self-enveloped universe" that attempts to "substitute fiction or signification for instances of the real."[9] Philosophy is a logical automaton through which "sign/thought/truth is indistinguishable from the real and usurps its position."[10] To forestall this usurpation of instances of the real, Kolozova follows Laruelle's non-philosophical method, which "operates with the 'transcendental material' of philosophy but without the amphibology in question."[11]

Kolozova's reduction of language to a technological automaton radically challenges a certain strain of poststructuralist dogma. She insists on the importance of situating the physical and language on "two different planes."[12] She thereby resists a kind of easy-going pan-textualism of the kind that institutionalized poststructuralism imagines. Kolozova insists on the non-exchangeability of sign and physicality. For Kolozova, there is a radical "opposition between the real insofar as physicality and the automaton of signification" that corresponds to the "immanent and the transcendental respectively."[13] The transcendental plane of signification is teleologically oriented toward the liquidation of the physical. Under the ideal (and idealist) hegemony of the empire of the sign, physicality "is to be used up completely in order to be transformed into pure value."[14] The signification machine or automaton—regardless of what language it operates in—is operationalized to substitute for the actual and the physical.

The logic of substitution immanent to language is benign in some instances. But the language or "automaton of capital" is anything but benign.[15] It has culminated (as Baudrillard intimated in 1972) in an economy of sign production in which physical labor and working bodies are abstracted into floating signs of exchange. The "automaton of capital or the tautological machine of pure value," writes Kolozova, "becomes gradually independent from its physical support and thus not only money but also [the] actual commodity become superfluous as in the case of the finance industry."[16] Here again Kolozova and the early Baudrillard are affine. Both see that late capital—the reign of the finance industry over the "real" economy—is the reign of the sign whose economic sovereignty annihilates the physical by expunging it from the system of pure value (or sign) exchange. The finance industry doesn't trade things—physical commodities—but purely speculative entities composed of pure value. The imperative of sign-based capital (or the automaton of capital) is holocaustal. But this is also true of standard philosophy. Hence, capitalism plus philosophy or supercapitalism is ethically marked by the "destruction of physicality" and of "brute materiality or animality."[17] Anything that contains "too much residual" physicality must be annihilated from the sphere of pure value.[18] This is the "main concern of capitalism, its teleology, and theology."[19]

Critique of (Financial) Speculation

Kolozova powerfully deploys her critique of speculation in her reading of the 2008 financial crash. The 2008 crash was a kind of revenge of the physical. The cycle of speculation on highly complexified "financial instruments" foundered on the shoals of real places, things, and bodies. Homes and workers—"toxic assets" as our economic "thought leaders" called them—was an instance of the real that interrupted the smooth white noise of neoliberal formalism.

The 2008 state intervention, the "bailout," was designed to save the speculative class. But the bailout "could not, however, be speculative," notes Kolozova.[20] "It had to draw on the material resources of its citizens: defaulted mortgages in the United States and austerity cuts in the EU. This brute material had to enter the scene of finances."[21] The return of the repressed, of disavowed physicality, had to step in to save speculation. It is always to the lives and livelihoods of the underclass that capitalism turns to save itself and reconsolidate its authority. "The material, in the guise of defaulted mortgages and destroyed livelihoods," writes Kolozova, "provided the grounds for the resurrection of a universe of nothing but signification—of finances and the speculative 'finance industry'."[22]

The 2008 financial meltdown demonstrated with brute ferocity the gap between what economists call the "real" economy and the financial sector. "The 2008 crisis was the first instance in the history of capitalism," writes Kolozova, "when the speculative foundation was proven untenable unless supported by matter and, in the last instance, determined by the real and/or physical."[23] Not only were the financiers rudely awakened from their speculative slumbers, so too were bourgeois economists. The latter simply could not speak intelligibly about physical things, laboring bodies, or life in general for that matter. The 2008 crash was also a crisis in standard economic theory. Because contemporary "economics is the product of philosophical determination in the last instance," writes Kolozova, "brute material is meaningless unless signified as monetary value."[24] The inability of bourgeois economic theory to theorize the physical is a symptom of the automaton of standard philosophy, which cannot intelligently capture any phenomena beyond pure conceptual logic. It can conceptualize materialism, but it knows nothing of the material *qua* physical. The automaton of signification (in its various forms) must be theoretically resisted by recalling and privileging what is exterminated by its logic—the physical—in order finally to destroy "the dictatorship of speculation in contemporary financial capitalism, postmodern theory, and politics."[25] Here we see the radical edge of the Kolozovan variant. It calls for a radical critique of the empire of the sign whose dominion extends over the economy in the form of pure value (or pure sign) exchange, in the form of textualism in postmodern theory, and in the form of "representation" in liberal politics.

Instances of the Real

Kolozova radicalizes the non-Marxist project by prizing physicality as an "instance of the real" resistant to supercapitalist abstraction.[26] "Instance of the real," is Kolozova's clone of the Laruellean "Real." The Real for Laruelle is a bar that he will not *theoretically* cross. Kolozova does not trespass on the Real either. But she does speak of "instances" and "cuts" of the "real."[27] Kolozova consistently writes "real" with a lowercase "r." This helps to distinguish it from Laruelle's formulation. But it also rhetorically serves Kolozova's conceptual purposes. She avoids sliding into a conception of the Real as a "totality," which is an entirely philosophical concept. Her formulation of "instances of the real" indicates that there are multiple ways that the real *qua* physical manifests.[28] Kolozova forestalls the establishment of "the real" as a transcendental signified in the traditional philosophical sense. She thereby elides a confusion that has dogged many of Laruelle's readers.

The instances of the real that Kolozova are most concerned with are, again, instances of physicality. Here there is an affinity with Henry's work. As we have seen, Henry attempts to ground Marxism on the reality lived life. But we should note the difference between Henry and Kolozova. Henry privileges the phenomenological "given" of the body. Kolozova takes nothing concerning physicality as *philosophically given*. She also does not restrict her concept of physicality to embodied humanness. Instances of the real *qua* physicality are "devoid of signification," philosophical or otherwise. Philosophy is a system of signification, which is to say a system of language. Philosophical language that claims to know the Real is always already the claim to know it systematically for language is systematic. But the physical *qua* real is different according to Kolozova. Instances of physicality "regardless of whether living or not, synthetic or artificial, if devoid of signification," writes Kolozova, "assumes the status of the real—that which escapes language, meaning, sense, which is the unruly, the absurd, the *unheimlich* (uncanny and outlandish), out-there."[29]

Kolozova's concept of the real as that which "escapes language" is clearly affine with Jacques Lacan's famed concept of the Real, which for him is the traumatic kernel that escapes understanding by language. But what is different is that Kolozova does not confine her concept of the real *qua* physicality to the *psychoanalytic concept* of trauma. Kolozova does not disagree in principle with the psychoanalytic tradition—indeed, she frequently draws upon its raw materials as does Laruelle—but she holds that the theoretical language of psychoanalysis *is precisely a language* that as such can never conceptually enclose the real *qua* physicality. Kolozova's concept of "instances of the real" provides a much-needed theoretical corrective within non-philosophy. By pluralizing and physicalizing Laruelle's concept of the Real, Kolozova radically resituates the non-Marxist project within a physical problematic and thereby demythologizes a certain reading of the Laruellean Real. This is to say only, but importantly, that the Kolozovan corrective remodels non-philosophy by reading it according to its immanent logic and not merely to its letter. Instances of the real *qua* physicality clones the Marxian primacy of materiality whereby the physical is rendered as non-philosophical in the last instance. This enables the concept to remain open to non-signifying instances of physicality whilst remaining rigorous enough to do meaningful theoretical work. Kolozova writes:

> The real is a status or mode of reality; it is not a self-standing concept as it must be determined by different and endless configurations of material reality. The clone is then determined by the real as matter, physicality, or abstraction that affects the thinking and/or the signifying automaton as an instance of the real, involving some materiality or material effectuation.[30]

The real as such never touches us, according to Kolozova, because there is no *real as such—no transcendental* totality—but only *instances of the real* that puncture the rationalizing schemas of standard philosophy, capitalism, natural and computational languages, and other modes of thinking axiomatically structured according to the principles of exchange and equivalence.[31] The *radicality of the Real* (*pace* Laruelle) or *instances of the real* (*pace* Kolozova) name what is indifferent to thought. This conception of the Real (or instances thereof) as radical indifference to thought resonates with Henry's axiomatic formulation: "Thought cannot do anything against reality."[32] Kolozova agrees in principle but she, contra Henry, does not look to philosophy as such to escape the impasse of idealism and the valorization of philosophical value. Instead, she formalizes philosophical thought in order to mount a critique against the empire of philosophical, financial, and patriarchal speculation in order to expose and destroy its epistemic domination.

Formalization

Kolozova's non-philosophical work (like that of Laruelle's) "requires the mobilization of philosophical material."[33] The material of philosophy is language. Hence, her defetishization of philosophy is in practice a defetishization of language. Kolozova affirms the structuralist insight that the structures and rules of languages or signification systems are contingently conditioned by the vicissitudes of their own historical-material development. All signification systems "arise from the conditioning necessity of the material and is bounded by its limitations."[34] Language systems are physically constrained, for example, by the range of vocal chords or the processing power of computers. There is always a physical basis that determines and limits the system. A signifying system can be formalized; its structures and rules laid bare and systematically deployed. But formalizing a signifying system, notes Kolozova, will not yield "an image of 'the truth of being' or a 'reflection on the real' (in the form of a philosophical truth of it)."[35] What formalization can do is yield the truth of the physical and material nature of a signifying system by plainly demonstrating that the system is "the result of the syntactic possibilities conditioned by the physical reality or the materiality of the machine."[36]

Formalization, for Kolozova, is a process of non-philosophical theorizing that divests philosophical language of its philosophically decisionist pretensions in order to recover it as material and physical. Non-philosophy in its various forms—non-Marxism, non-aesthetics, non-photography, and so on—are models for "prospective formal languages of post-philosophy" that "allow for poesy while being scientifically rigorous."[37] Kolozova argues that the languages of "post-philosophy" are cloned versions of the language games of standard philosophy but with their decisionist pretensions voided. Kolozova's conception of post-philosophical language takes a lesson from the poets. We should as non-philosophers defetishize language, but in that discover the potentialities that language has as a material and develop and deploy those potentialities in a "scientifically rigorous" manner.

Kolozova clearly distinguishes her method of formalization from that of Laruelle's method of cloning. "Procedurally, the following would be an operation of cloning," writes Kolozova: "concepts as signifiers (meaning parts of language rather than a doctrine) [are] taken from the disassembled *chôra* of philosophical systems."[38] This procedure of cloning she takes from Laruelle. But Kolozova radically and concretely develops what Laruelle only schematically names "syntax of the Real." Cloning is supposed to "mimic the Real" without claiming epistemic access to it.[39] But Laruelle really does not spell out how this works. Kolozova does. "Laruelle does not refer to the notion of structure," writes Kolozova, "nor does he explain more specifically the concept of the 'syntax of the real.' Yet ... we can safely claim that the notion of 'syntax' can refer only to a structure of signification."[40] That is, the "syntax of the Real" must mimic the Real in the translational and material space of language. The Real is cloned in the syntax of non-philosophy. This is most apparent in the vexing problem of prepositional language such as in the clone "force-(of)-thought." There is no "of" thought since thought is "in" the Real. Yet within the schismatic language of philosophy, we are forced to work (sometimes awkwardly) in such a way to render in syntax the axiom that all thought is always already in and determined by the Real in the last instance. Formalization, for Kolozova, enables one to "intellectually grasp" the radicality of the Real by dint of the insufficiency of the non-philosophical clone. What Kolozova calls her "formalism of materialist reason" will "permit and acknowledge the remainder that escapes signification," which is to say all *instances of the real*.[41] Kolozova's "formalism of materialist reason" dethrones the vaunted philosophical concept of "reason" by formally cloning it in the insufficient material of language. This finally yields a radically non-philosophical and materialist conception of language. "Language is technology," writes Kolozova, "and technology is *techné*, not *philosophia*."[42] Language is treated as technical, practical, and material, not as philosophical, not as transcendental with respect to the Real or instances of it. Language "exacts operations over and through the physical, not in order to 'transcend it,'" writes Kolozova, but rather so it can be used "in ways that help weighed-down animals, including human animals in the physical reality they inhabit."[43] Kolozova argues that language is an "automaton" inasmuch as it operates in a machinic manner and it can "transcend" certain physical limits—written signs can outlive the body who inscribes them—but at the same time it is grounded in radically physical needs. Our own physical constraints as animals require linguistic technologies to transcend those constraints. Kolozova importantly gives us a theoretical model of language at once immanent, physical, and transcendental, but radically determined by the physical *qua* instance of the real. Contra, the agency of the "philosophical fetish" of the *thinker*, Kolozova gives us the "agency of *techné*" as the "automaton (of signification) moved by the needs of species-being."[44]

The Dyadic Self

Kolozova's privileging of physicality opens a site of critical resistance against the annihilatory strategies of standard philosophy, capitalism, and patriarchy. In this respect, it complements and develops intersectional feminist struggles against capitalist-patriarchy. The theoretical infrastructure of the Kolozovan variant enables a unique theorization of "selfhood" as the non-synthetic or non-amphibological conjoining of physicality with the automaton of language. Kolozova writes:

> We have called this reality of selfhood the non-human; the interstice is insurmountable; the physical and the automaton are one under the identity in the last instance but a unification does not take place. At the heart of it there is something that escapes sense – it can be intellectually grasped, it can be "described" or cloned … but it escapes reason and its human shape (philosophy).[45]

Kolozova strategically marshals a wholly generic concept of "selfhood"—irreducible to humanness or philosophies of humanism—the identity of which incorporates without sublating the difference between physicality and the automaton of language. Kolozova constructs her model of selfhood in part by using the raw materials provided by Donna Haraway's theory of the "cyborg."[46] Haraway famously turned to the figure of the cyborg as a means to conceptualize figures of humanness, machinery, animality, and women without submitting to the binary logic of "nature" or "culture." Kolozova radicalizes Haraway's theoretical figure. The cyborg for Kolozova is neither a synthesis of nature and culture, nor its deconstruction, but a figure that allegorizes the non-coincidence and radical non-alignment of these two elements or instances. "I read Donna Haraway's concept of the 'cyborg,'" writes Kolozova, "as fundamentally the product of a non-philosophical procedure of dualysis brought about by radicalizing the dyad [of the automaton of language and that of the physical body], rendering its two constituents irreducible to one another."[47]

The heart of Kolozova's theory of cyborg selfhood "escapes sense" even while it can be "intellectually grasped." It "escapes sense" inasmuch as it is an instance of "identity" without unification. This can be "intellectually grasped" with generic formulations such as "identity" as the instance of "nonidentity" to put the matter in Adornian terms. But to *intellectually grasp* selfhood as the non-coincidence of language and physicality is not the same thing as *making philosophical sense* of it. For Kolozova, no model of selfhood can philosophically integrate the function of language with the experience of physicality without producing an idealist (and idealized) model of selfhood according to the philosophical imperatives of egoism. Precisely because it cannot be signified sensibly it constitutes an "instance of the real" in the Kolozovan variant.

Egoistic models of selfhood invariably reproduce some version of Cartesian man: the "I" that is identical to the saying of "I." From this egoistical point of philosophical self-assurance has flowed a world of hurt and domination under the veil of reason. Kolozova's conception of selfhood as the non-identity of physicality and language "escapes signification," which is to say that it is an "instance of the real." In Kolozova's model, selfhood, at "its heart" is not a philosophical concept: it is an "instance of the real" to which philosophy must yield its sovereignty and for which we must politically struggle. We have therefore a *theory* (a means of intellectually grasping) selfhood as that which in the last instance is an instance of the real. To theorize this nonidentical heart of selfhood requires a "dualysis"—a mode of non-philosophical analysis—which considers each element, in this case that of the physical and the automaton of language, as irreducible to one another or to any mixture of the two and yet, because it is "real," is also "one" in the last instance. The Kolozovan model intellectually grasps selfhood as "one" *qua* non-synthesizable two.

Against Sacrifice and Martyrdom

Kolozova's insistence on the radicality of the physical is marshaled into a theoretical mode of working in which the raw materials of philosophy—and the automaton of signification generally—are used to illuminate and radicalize the gap between the real *qua* physical and signification. This has not only theoretical, but political consequences. In her opposition to the reign of the sign in postmodern theory, Kolozova reminds us of the destroyed bodies and places that serve as the disavowed supports for the transcendence of the sign in theory and in economic practice.

"Theory" in the Kolozovan variant is the elaboration, development, and deployment of the raw materials provided by philosophy and the material resources provided by the automaton of language in service to the defetishization of speculation and a means to establish solidarity with all animals (human and non-human alike) who are victimized and annihilated by the supercapitalist logic that iteratively reproduces the valorization of value at the expense of bodies.

It is clear today, in the teeth of COVID-19, an economic catastrophe, and the continued state-sponsored killing of Black people, that capitalism is a sacrificial economy. The annihilatory and racist logic of supercapitalism is brutally clear. And it is not only the capitalist class, those shades that haunt Wall Street, who must be held accountable; *the capitalist philosophers must also be counted among the guilty*. Our economic departments, think tanks, and the like must be brought to justice. This must mean reparations, redistribution and reallocation as well as a wholesale reconstruction of social values. Witness the poverty of our "philosophy" in the United States: we are being asked to choose either to sacrifice our fellow human beings and "save the economy" or to face certain "ruin." But a system that can only "think" in terms of killing or of making a killing is not worth saving. We must kill that system else we kill ourselves. This is the radical edge of the Kolozovan variant. It makes us face the genocidal core of supercapitalism.

Non-Marxist theory is a political engagement inasmuch as it fights against supercapitalism. Its principal strategy is to clone philosophy in such a way that its determination by the Real in the last instance is manifest at the discursive and conceptual levels. "Those who wish to subscribe to some of the central tenets of this theory and wish to escape the circularity and auto-referentiality of philosophy," writes Kolozova, "should theorize in a way in which thought succumbs to the authority of the real."[48] Theory that "succumbs to the authority of the real," for Kolozova, requires theorizing "in a way" that "succumbs" to ethically urgent instances of physical suffering. "The urgency to cease the suffering of the tormented body," writes Kolozova, must be theoretically answered by a gesture that will "burst asunder the mirror-world of surplus value, that universe of pure abstraction and operations of speculation called capitalism."[49] To "burst asunder the mirror-world of surplus value" requires a break with supercapitalist thinking, but it also requires breaking the hallucinations of philosophical Marxism, including a political break with the allure of the sacrificial economy of communism as we have known it. Kolozova writes:

> Martyrdom is a theological and philosophical value, not a communist one. Communism is radically democratic. The Leninist and post-Leninist legacy of communism has instituted it as a form of Abrahamic theology, of self-sacrifice and sacrifices, of martyrdom and physical suffering in the name of a grand idea. The theology of this tradition ... is hateful of democracy ... It is hateful of the idea that everyone is equally competent enough to participate in the building of a just society. It is also hateful of

the bodily ..., [of the] mortal body, and its finality vis-à-vis the immortality of the great idea.[50]

Non-Marxism ethically requires a commitment to the democratic principle that all are accorded a presumption of equal competence to the production of a just society. This requires that no idea be fetishized and reified as *the* answer. For non-philosophy, "all thought is equal," as O'Maoilearca has powerfully put it, in that no thought can be held to be decisive for that would simply usurp the radicality of the Real and the decisiveness it exercises in the last instance. All thought, including non-Marxism and its variants, must succumb to instances of the real and work to establish in thought the non-dictatorship of what Marx called the "general intellect." Theory can participate in this general intellectual work by radicalizing its structurally necessitated metaphysical dimension. It is to this metaphysical dimension of the Kolozovan variant that I now turn.

Radical Metaphysics

I first encountered Kolozova's work on metaphysics with a sense of surprise. Why should metaphysics play any role in a theoretical mode that is intellectually and politically determined by the real and the physical? What could be more "philosophical" and less physical than metaphysics and how could that possibly be accommodated to non-Marxism's drive to philosophically impoverish Marxism? The answer lies in the matter of estrangement. For Kolozova, estrangement is a metaphysical process. Kolozova writes:

The real of the human ... according to Laruelle's non-analysis, inevitably mediates itself through a process of estranging oneself from the real that one is. One has to transpose oneself into a lingually conceived self, into a subject, in order to mediate the real (one is) to the others and to oneself. Prior to becoming a subject one becomes a "Stranger," which is "radical subjectivity." ... [T]he Stranger is affected by the immanence of the process of estrangement. It is concrete, made of transcendental material (language), and is in unilateral affirmation of the dyad ... of the real and the transcendental (language) ... The Stranger is still in the real (of estrangement) while the trauma of the primal metaphysical procedure takes place – that of "becoming a stranger to oneself" or sensing the core of oneself as an exteriority. Laruelle insists that the "concreteness" of the Stranger is not "empirico-metaphysical," but rather "transcendental." My claim is that this gesture is fundamentally metaphysical.[51]

In other words, the non-exchangeability and non-equivalence between the lived experience of physicality and language induces a process of self-estrangement—the becoming-stranger—of subjectification. The concrete production of the concrete stranger as subject is experienced as the exteriorization of oneself. Metaphysical thought is rooted in this experience of estrangement. Self-estrangement is induced by the diremption between physical experience and grammar (or rules) of language. To confront oneself as a stranger induces one to ask questions like: Who am I? What is real or really important? These questions are not only abstract and transcendental: they are symptomatic of physical life. "The subject constituting process of estrangement is a sensation," notes

Kolozova, "as it involves physicality and intense mental experience which precedes pure concept, but nonetheless represents a process of conceptualization."[52] The subjectification process "is an experience of anxiety, pain, and pleasure."[53] This physical-cognitive experience precedes the constitution of a "pure concept" of estrangement, but insofar as this experience is in part a mental experience, it constitutes a "process of conceptualization," which is to say a process of thought. Despite the fact that the generic human is "in" the real in the last instance, the estranging process of subjectification brings about an experience of oneself as an exteriority or outside the Real.

"Philosophy does not precede metaphysics," writes Kolozova, "but it is rather the other way around."[54] Metaphysics is not a philosophical matter in the first instance. It has been converted into a *philosophical subject*, but this conversion into the pure value of philosophical logic does not capture the physical basis of metaphysical questions. "The metaphysical question is in the last instance prelingual," writes Kolozova.[55]

Metaphysical thought is structurally determined by instances of the real of physical life. This in brief is the radical kernel of Kolozovan metaphysics. Kolozova radically differentiates her project from the standard post-Heideggerian philosophical project of "the overcoming of metaphysics." The aim to overcome metaphysics, according to Kolozova, is simply another instance of how the logic of philosophical-capitalist thought seeks to annihilate the physical. Kolozova writes:

> My claim is that there is no escape from metaphysics. We are metaphysical creatures inasmuch as we are material ones, with the

latter always already inviting the former. However, an exit from the disciplining and hallucinatory grasp of philosophical metaphysics is possible, as both Marx and Laruelle have shown.[56]

Kolozova fetishizes neither metaphysics nor its overcoming. Metaphysics is cloned to re-emphasize the "physical" element of metaphysics. We should rethink metaphysics at the level of physically lived life rather than project it into a heaven of philosophy or fetishize it as a monstrous Goliath that must be brought down. All attempts to provide a *philosophy of metaphysics* are trapped in a dialectical dead end. Either philosophy is presented as the final word on what is real (classical metaphysics) or philosophy is presented as an immanent replacement for it (the critique of metaphysics). Kolozovan metaphysics is radical and immanent. Here it is instructive to turn to the work of Rocco Gangle to help flesh out the radicality of immanent metaphysics.

In his path-breaking work, *Diagrammatic Immanence*, Gangle argues for a decisively differential cut between immanent metaphysics and ontology. There is an understandable slippage and confusion between the terms "metaphysics" and "ontology" since both are commonly used to refer to philosophies that claim to know reality at its most fundamental. To an extent then the confusion is not only understandable but logically justified. But "immanent metaphysics" logically cancels out the possibility of ontology. "If immanence is how reality is ultimately structured," writes Gangle, "then ontology is ineluctably constrained to relations. Things must be relations 'all the way down' (however far that is) without remainder."[57] Radical immanence is incompatible with an ontology of "things" because the logic of things presupposes that there are not only immanent relations but *entities* that determine the mode of immanent relations and are therefore logically prior to immanent relations and therefore ultimately not immanent in the last instance. If immanence "is correct metaphysically speaking," writes Gangle, "then '[t]hings' in the usual sense are ultimately no more than relations of some kind or another that hold or do not hold among other sorts of relations, and so on."[58] Gangle's key insight enables us to further distinguish Kolozova's radical metaphysics from standard post-Heideggerian philosophy. Physicality is not a "physical thing" in the empirical sense for Kolozova. It is a mode of relationality that bears the impress or the "cut of the Real." Questions of a traditionally metaphysical kind are, for Kolozova, the estranged refraction of this radically immanent modality of physicality. Physicality is more than what is empirically counted as physical: it is metaphysical in that sense.

Kolozova calls for the recommencement of metaphysics from a radically immanent and physical perspective. The question of metaphysics is redirected by Kolozova to what precedes philosophical questioning. But to achieve this "one has to step out of philosophy's circularity and submit to the particular metaphysical reality as an instance of the real and materiality."[59] "Metaphysical reality" sounds almost like a paradox, but this quasi-paradox is an index of the radically physical basis of metaphysical questioning. Prior to the emergence of metaphysical questions is the experience of radical diremption between the physical body and the annihilatory logic that underwrites its conversion of the physical into an automaton of signification. The "metaphysical," notes Kolozova, is marked by immanent estrangement, a "struggle with the real and the possibility of detachment of the spectral self from the real."[60] Estrangement is an "experience of anxiety, pain, and pleasure," which as "experience [is] a pure instance of the lived (Laruelle) of the real."[61] In a remarkable and radical move Kolozova steals back metaphysics from the logic of Philosophical Decision and thus from the anti-physical automaton of standard philosophy. The Kolozovan variant enables a radical recommencement of metaphysics from the perspective of the actual, the physical, and the experiential yielding for us a new conception of metaphysics. The standard conception of metaphysics as transcendent is a philosophical cult-image whose economic double is the financial industry. Radical metaphysics of the Kolozovan variant is metaphysics submitted to the *diktat* of the radical physicality *qua* instance of the real.

7

Conclusion

Through a series of constellations—stranger, struggle, impossibilization, fiction, and metaphysics—this book has attempted to trace what I take to be some of the key points of reference and departure for doing Marxism otherwise than philosophically in the standard sense. We began by a brief setting of the scene of the non-Marxist challenge as the challenge to think philosophy otherwise than according to the principles of exchange and equivalence that underwrite philosophy and capitalism or supercapitalism. How can we think philosophically without entering into or affirming a system that is premised on the ideology that the Real can be exchanged for its equivalent in concepts like the way bread and money are made seemingly fungible in market life? Marx indicated for us a path to an exit from philosophy, but he demonstrated that the exit was more like a corridor of indeterminate length which had to be passed through. Marx's passage through philosophy was (*pace* Labica) a "necessary sojourn" inasmuch as no exit from philosophy could even be attempted in anything but a vulgar, anti-intellectual manner unless the limits of philosophical reason were theoretically demonstrated in the context of a political project of radical emancipation.

Laruelle follows Marx in warning us that one cannot simply declare philosophy dead or irrelevant for practical and political reasons without risking either a repetition of an already hackneyed history of such declarations by philosophers or, more problematically, without risking the possibility that in that imagined "exit" from philosophy, one simply affirms a certain logical structure that decides the Real. Laruelle's approach to the exit from "Marxist philosophy" sends us back to philosophy, but in a way that estranges philosophical materials by treating them as materials rather than doctrinal decisions on the Real. Marx's theory of "estrangement" is cloned and transformed into a "stranger-Subject" for a "stranger Marxism" than we have known. This stranger Marxism enables another means of salvaging (via cloning) the concept of the radicality of the individual (*pace* Henry) without affirming the philosophies of the human, including anti-humanism, posthumanism, and so forth. I stress that non-Marxism's reformulation of estrangement and what Laruelle calls the "finite individual" operate as "purely" conceptual operators strangely in order to show what resists purely philosophical conceptualization. Yet at the same time, this "purely" conceptual status of the non-philosophical cloning is also entirely material inasmuch as it is "reduces" philosophy to materials.

We then turned to the important question of struggle in Marxist philosophy. Here we situated Laruelle's project between two poles of Marxist theory of the 1960s, namely, the primacy of theory and the primacy of practice. We allegorized this tension by the names Althusser (primacy of theory) and Tronti (primacy of practice) in order to show what aspects of non-Marxism remain within the theoretical ambit of each. Non-Marxism, however, rejects the theoreticist program of the early Althusser (and arguably the later), and it resists the positivist concept of the "proletariat" we find in Tronti. Instead, it dualyzes the relation between theoretical and political practice and constitutes a "non-proletarian" *qua* "subject-in-struggle" that struggles against the annihilatory abstractions of philosophy and capitalism in the name of the "Victim-in-person" and the Real in the last instance.

Following our "necessary sojourn" within the matrix of Marxist philosophy's struggle over the question of struggle, we turned to non-Marxism's (and non-philosophy's) affinities with structuralism. Descombes importantly reminds us that structuralism has never meant in practice anything like affirmations of the whole or totality. It emphasizes instead the discrete isomorphic relations that hold across discrete phenomena. "Structure" names only this partial isomorphism. It stresses that only these partial structures can be usefully analyzed. Structuralism teaches us that there is little to nothing to say about wholes or totalities. I have argued that Laruelle's thesis on Philosophical Decision is a structuralist thesis. Operationalizing a certain structuralist orientation, I tried to show how we might usefully describe certain affinities between Adorno's project of negative dialectics and non-philosophy. Adorno teaches us to reckon with how concepts fail to capture what they claim to capture whereas Laruelle teaches us that all philosophies (positive or negative dialectics and so on) fail to decide on the Real despite their implicit or explicit decisionist claims. This "negative" perspective allows us to reclaim a concept of the "ordinary" individual as that which appears "mystical" from the standpoint of supercapitalism. The individual, for Laruelle, is what cannot be reduced to the infinite calculus of fungibility prized by supercapitalism. Finally, we saw that the aim of non-Marxism is to render Marxism truly unworkable or impossible according to the principles of exchange and equivalence that underwrites the logic of standard philosophy.

We then turned to the question of what form non-Marxism might take via a reading of the status of "fiction" in the work of Laruelle and Baudrillard. Baudrillard and Laruelle start out from affine positions on the Real. For Baudrillard, the Real has disappeared from the horizon of thinkability in the age of the hyperreal, whereas for Laruelle, the Real cannot be decided except in the form of a philosophical hallucination of decision. In response both thinkers turned to the conceptual and rhetorical resources of fiction in order to refashion Marxian theory in non-dialectical terms that cancel in advance the principles of exchange and equivalence that underwrite the supercapitalist political economy of thought.

Finally, we turned to the what I call the "Kolozovan variant," which represents a major development within the theory of non-Marxism. Kolozova recasts metaphysics as a structurally necessary point of departure within the non-Marxist conjuncture. Crucially, Kolozova locates metaphysics within the most ordinary and human of questions. Metaphysics is not for her the vaunted work of trained philosophers only. It is the ordinary habit of posing questions that spring from the annihilatory logic of philosophy and capital. Philosophy and capital's drive to annihilate physicality *qua* instance of the real conditions the radical estrangement of physical life from the logic of abstraction. The Kolozovan variant yields a profound insight: *metaphysics is fundamentally a physical problem.*

Coda

As I write these words, the death toll from COVID-19 in the United States continues to rise. The Trump administration's political project is to abstract away death. But the bodies are piling up nonetheless. In the face of this: what is the point of doing theory? What is the point in writing a book like this? I think it is wrong to "defend" theory by way of the suffering of others. Theory does not end suffering. But still we might consider the very act of doing theory as a protest against a world that every minute demands that our actions be productive and have a real return on investment. To do theory is to think about thinking and to do this is to refuse to think toward immediate and tangible ends. It is, indeed, to think in a mediated way through the medium of theory itself.[1] This attenuated form of thinking that we call "theory" remains important today even (or especially) in the teeth of the imperative to act. How can we justify a project of such apparent abstraction that nonetheless claims a fidelity to all that is Real in the last instance? We cannot. At least we cannot do so in any way that would not be itself philosophical. We say with Althusser that we are necessarily "committed to a theoretical destiny."[2] We must necessarily "sojourn in philosophy" (*pace* Labica) because there is no easy exit from philosophy except by means that are too often themselves philosophical in the last instance. To think non-philosophically is to think against philosophy's authority and its authoritarian impulses. And in that sense to think non-philosophically is not a retreat into mere thinking. It is a resistance to the logic of domination in thought in radical fidelity to the defense of a democracy-in-thought.

NOTES

Chapter 1

1 The term "non-standard philosophy" is less misleading than "non-philosophy." But the latter term (for better and for worse) is better known and it is the one I use.

2 François Laruelle, *Struggle and Utopia at the End Times of Philosophy*, trans. Drew S. Burk and Anthony Paul Smith (Minneapolis: Univocal Publishing, 2012), 28.

3 Louis Althusser, *For Marx*, trans. Ben Brewster (New York: Vintage Books, 1970), 113.

4 François Laruelle, *Principles of Non-Philosophy*, trans. Nicola Rubczak and Anthony Paul Smith (London: Bloomsbury Academic, 2013), 146.

5 See Rocco Gangle, Unpublished Draft. At the time of this writing, Gangle's paper is in draft form and not yet published. A version of it is set to be published in the forthcoming edition of the *Oxford Handbook of French Philosophy*.

6 Laruelle, *Struggle and Utopia at the End Times of Philosophy*, 29.

7 Ibid.

8 John Mullarkey, *Post-Continental Philosophy: An Outline* (London: Continuum, 2006), 137. Note that the author now goes by the name John O'Maoilearca.

9 François Laruelle, *Introduction to Non-Marxism*, trans. Anthony Paul Smith (Minneapolis: Univocal Publishing, 2015), 169.

10 Ibid., 80.

11 Ibid., 81.

12 Ibid.

13 Ibid.

14 Ibid., 1.

15 Ibid., 2.

16 Ibid.

17 Walter Benjamin, *The Origin of German Tragic Drama*, trans. George Osborne (London: Verso, 2009), 34.

18 Theodor W. Adorno, *Negative Dialectics*, trans. E.B. Ashton (New York: Continuum, 1973), 11.

19 Ibid., 11.

20 Ibid.

21 Ibid., 163.

22 Laruelle, *Principles of Non-Philosophy*, 7.

23 Ibid., 7.

Chapter 2

1 John O'Maoilearca, *All Thoughts Are Equal: Laruelle and Non-Human Philosophy* (Minneapolis: University of Minnesota Press, 2015), 1.

2 Ibid.

3 Ibid., 2–3.

4 Ibid., 6.

5 Ibid.

6 William James, *Pragmatism: A New Name for Some Old Ways of Thinking* (London: Longmans, Green, and Co., 1907), 6.

7 Anthony Paul Smith, *Laruelle: A Stranger Thought* (Cambridge: Polity Press, 2016), 80.

8 O'Maoilearca, *All Thoughts Are Equal*, 6.

9 Laruelle, *Introduction to Non-Marxism*, 7.

10 Katerina Kolozova, *Capitalism's Holocaust of Animals: A Non-Marxist Critique of Capital, Philosophy, and Patriarchy* (London: Bloomsbury Academic, 2020), 6.

11 Laruelle, *Struggle and Utopia at the End Times of Philosophy*, 38.

12 Althusser, *For Marx*, 158–159.

13 Karl Marx, *Economic and Philosophic Manuscripts of 1844* (Moscow: Progress Publishers, 1974), 63.

14 Ibid., 65–66.

15 Michel Henry, *Marx: An Introduction*, trans. Kristien Justaert (London: Bloomsbury Academic, 2019), 10.

16 Ibid., 11.

17 Ibid.

18 Ibid.

19 Ibid., 12.

20 François Laruelle, *A Biography of Ordinary Man: On Authorities and Minorities*, trans. Jesse Hock and Alex Dubilet (Cambridge: Polity Press, 2018), 10.

21 François Laruelle and Collaborators, *Dictionary of Non-Philosophy*, trans. Taylor Adkins (Minneapolis: Univocal Publishing, 2013), 143.

22 Karl Marx and Friedrich Engels, *The German Ideology: Parts I and II*, ed. R. Pascal (New York: International Publishers, 1960), 4.

23 Ibid., 6.

24 Karl Marx, *Theses on Feuerbach*, in *The German Ideology*, 197.

25 Étienne Balibar, *The Philosophy of Marx*, trans. Chris Turner and Gregory Elliott (London: Verso, 2017), 17.

26 Ibid., 19.

27 Georges Labica, *Marxism and the Status of Philosophy*, trans. Kate Soper and Martin Ryle (Sussex: The Harvester Press, 1980), 67.

28 Ibid.

29 Ibid., 69.

30 Karl Marx, *The Poverty of Philosophy* (New York: International Publishers, 1982), 29.

31 Labica, *Marxism and the Status of Philosophy*, 145.

32 Henry, *Marx*, 19–20.

33 Gregory Elliott, *Althusser: The Detour of Theory* (Chicago: Haymarket Books, 2009), 73.

34 See O' Maoilearca, *All Thoughts Are Equal*.

35 Laruelle and Collaborators, *Dictionary of Non-Philosophy*, 46.

36 Laruelle, *Struggle and Utopia at the End Times of Philosophy*, 30.

37 Ibid.

38 Laruelle, *Introduction to Non-Marxism*, 44.

39 Ibid.

40 Ibid., 137.

41 Ibid., 93.

42 Ibid., 37.

43 Ibid., 93.

44 Ibid.

45 Ibid.

46 Ibid.

47 François Laruelle, *The Concept of Non-Photography*, trans. Robin Mackay (New York: Urbanomic/Sequence Press, 2012), 2.

48 Ibid., 8.

49 Ibid., 56.

50 Ibid.

51 Mullarkey, *Post-Continental Philosophy*, 137.

52 See Jonathan Fardy, *Laruelle and Art: The Aesthetics of Non-Philosophy* (London: Bloomsbury Academic, 2020).

53 Mullarkey, *Post-Continental Philosophy*, 134.

54 Ibid.

55 Laruelle, *The Concept of Non-Photography*, 8.

56 From an online interview with Kolozova conducted by Jonathan Fardy.

57 Ibid.

58 Laruelle, *Introduction to Non-Marxism*, 3.

Chapter 3

1. François Laruelle, *Theory of Identities*, trans. Alyosha Edlebi (New York: Columbia University Press, 2016), 82.

2. Ibid.

3. Quoted in Louis Althusser et al., *Reading Capital: The Complete Edition*, trans. Ben Brewster and David Fernbach (London: Verso, 2015), 19.

4. Ibid., 20.

5. Ibid., 24.

6. Louis Althusser, *Philosophy and the Spontaneous Philosophy of the Scientists*, ed. Gregory Elliott, trans. Ben Brewster, James H. Kavanaugh, Thomas E. Lewis, Grahame Lock, and Warren Montag (New York: Verso, 1990), 15.

7. Laruelle, *Introduction to Non-Marxism*, 175.

8. Ibid.

9. E.P. Thompson, *The Poverty of Theory and Other Essays* (New York: Monthly Reviews Press, 1978), 8.

10. Jacques Rancière, *Althusser's Lesson*, trans. Emiliano Battista (London: Continuum, 2011), xvi.

11. Ibid.

12. Ibid., 10.

13. Laruelle, *Introduction to Non-Marxism*, 143.

14. Ibid.

15. Louis Althusser, *Essays in Self-Criticism*, trans. Grahame Lock (London: NLB, 1976), 68.

16. Ibid.

17. Ibid., 166.

18. Ibid.

19. Ibid.

20. Louis Althusser, *Lenin and Philosophy and Other Essays*, trans. Ben Brewster (New York: Monthly Review Press, 2001), 1.

21 Ibid., 2.

22 Elliott, *Althusser*, 178.

23 Althusser, *Lenin and Philosophy*, 8.

24 Ibid., 17.

25 Ibid.

26 Ibid.

27 Ted Benton, *The Rise and Fall of Structural Marxism: Althusser and His Influence* (New York: St. Martin's Press, 1984), 90.

28 Ibid.

29 Ibid., 91.

30 Ibid., 90.

31 Alain Badiou, *Metapolitics*, trans. Jason Barker (London: Verso, 2005), 61.

32 Ibid., 60.

33 Ibid., 61.

34 Ibid., 62.

35 Alain Badiou, *Philosophy for Militants*, trans. Bruno Bosteels (London: Verso, 2012), Kindle Edition, 13.

36 Badiou, *Metapolitics*, 62.

37 Mario Tronti, *Workers and Capital*, trans. David Broder (London: Verso, 2019), 31.

38 Ibid.

39 Ibid.

40 Ibid., 34.

41 Ibid., 27–28.

42 Étienne Balibar, "A Point of Heresy in Western Marxism: Althusser's and Tronti's Antithetic Readings of *Capital*," in *The Concept in Crisis: Reading Capital Today*, ed. Nick Nesbitt (Durham: Duke University Press, 2017), 107.

43 Ibid.

44 Laruelle, *Introduction to Non-Marxism*, 139.

45 Sara R. Farris, "Althusser and Tronti: The Primacy of Politics Versus the Autonomy of the Political," in *Encountering Althusser: Politics and Materialism in Contemporary Radical Thought*, eds. Katja Diefenbach, Sara R. Farris, Gal Kirn, and Peter D. Thomas (London: Bloomsbury Academic, 2013), 188.

46 Tronti, *Workers and Capital*, 3.

47 Farris, "Althusser and Tronti," 189.

48 Steve Wright, *Storming Heaven: Class Composition and Struggle in Italian Autonomist Marxism* (London: Pluto Press, 2017), 71.

49 Ibid., 37.

50 Tronti, *Workers and Capital*, 185.

51 Quoted in Ibid., 185.

52 Laruelle, *Introduction to Non-Marxism*, 189.

53 Ibid., 121–122.

54 See Alfred Sohn-Rethel, *Intellectual and Manual Labor: A Critique of Epistemology* (Atlantic Highlands: Humanities Press, 1978).

55 Laruelle, *Introduction to Non-Marxism*, 126.

56 Kolozova, *Capitalism's Holocaust of Animals*, 92.

57 Laruelle, *Introduction to Non-Marxism*, 166.

58 Alexander Galloway, *Laruelle: Against the Digital* (Minneapolis: University of Minnesota Press, 2014), 121.

59 Ibid., 120.

60 Laruelle, *Introduction to Non-Marxism*, 165.

61 Smith, *Laruelle*, 111.

62 Laruelle, *Introduction to Non-Marxism*, 165.

63 Ibid., 127.

64 Kolozova, *Capitalism's Holocaust of Animals*, 97.

65 François Laruelle, *General Theory of Victims*, trans. Jesse Hock and Alex Dubilet (Cambridge: Polity Press, 2015), 24.

66 See Francois Laruelle, *Anti-Badiou: On The Introduction of Maoism into Philosophy*, trans. Robin Mackay (London: Bloomsbury Academic, 2013).

67 Laruelle, *General Theory of Victims*, 18.

68 Ibid., xiii.

69 Ibid., xiii.

70 Ibid., xiv.

71 Ibid., 5.

72 Laruelle, *Introduction to Non-Marxism*, 133.

73 Ibid., 134.

74 Smith, *Laruelle*, 49.

75 Laruelle, *Introduction to Non-Marxism*, 134–135.

76 Ibid., 172–173.

77 See Jacques Derrida, *Specters of Marx: The State of Debt, the Work of Mourning, and the New International* (New York: Routledge, 2006).

78 Laruelle, *Introduction to Non-Marxism*, 3.

Chapter 4

1 Ian James, *The Technique of Thought: Nancy, Laruelle, Malabou, and Stiegler after Naturalism* (Minneapolis: University of Minnesota Press, 2019), 30.

2 Ibid.

3 One of the best historians of structuralism is undoubtedly François Dosse. See François Dosse, *History of Structuralism: The Rising of the Sign, 1945–1966 (Volume I)*, trans. Deborah Glassman (Minneapolis: University of Minnesota Press, 1998); and François Dosse, *History of Structuralism: The Sign Sets, 1967–Present (Volume II)*, trans. Deborah Glassman (Minneapolis: University of Minnesota Press, 1998).

4 Vincent Descombes, *Modern French Philosophy*, trans. L Scott-Fox and J. M. Harding (Cambridge: Cambridge University Press, 1980), 77.

5 Ibid., 84–85.

6 Ibid., 86.

7   Ibid., 87.
8   Laruelle, *Introduction to Non-Marxism*, 10.
9   Ibid., 7.
10 Ibid., 167.
11 Laruelle, *A Biography of Ordinary Man*, 73.
12 Ibid.
13 Michel Foucault, *The Order of Things: An Archaeology of the Human Sciences* (New York: Vintage Books, 1994), 387.
14 Henry, *Marx*, 11.
15 Ibid., 10.
16 Ibid., 12.
17 Ibid.
18 Ibid.
19 Ibid., 19.
20 Laruelle, *A Biography of Ordinary Man*, 70.
21 Ibid., 60.
22 Theodor Adorno, *Minima Moralia: Reflections from Damaged Life*, trans. E.F.N. Jephcott (New York: Verso, 2005), 39.
23 Edward W. Said, *Representation of the Intellectual* (New York: Vintage Books, 1994), 53.
24 Ibid., 57.
25 See Martin Jay, *Adorno* (Cambridge: Harvard University Press, 1984), 56.
26 Quoted in Geoff Boucher, *Adorno Reframed: Interpreting Key Thinkers for the Arts* (London: I.B. Tauris, 2013), 22–23.
27 Theodor W. Adorno, *Aesthetic Theory*, trans. Robert Hullot-Kentor (Minneapolis: University of Minnesota Press, 1997), 166.
28 Robert Hullot-Kentor, "Translator's Introduction," in Adorno, *Aesthetic Theory*, xiii.
29 Ibid., xx.
30 Adorno, *Negative Dialectics*, 4.

31 Hullot-Kentor, "Translator's Introduction," xi.

32 Adorno, *Negative Dialectics*, 5.

33 Ibid., 10.

34 Ibid., 5.

35 Ibid.

36 Ibid.

37 Ibid., 8.

38 Ibid., 6.

39 Ibid., 11.

40 Ibid.

41 Ibid.

42 Ibid., 10.

43 Ibid.

44 Fredric Jameson, *Late Marxism: Adorno or the Persistence of the Dialectic* (New York: Verso, 1990), 26.

45 Ibid.

46 Ibid., 23.

47 Adorno, *Negative Dialectics*, 11.

48 François Laruelle, *Photo-Fiction, a Non-Standard Aesthetics*, trans. Drew S. Burk (Minneapolis: Univocal Publishing, 2012), 18.

49 Laruelle and Collaborators, *Dictionary of Non-Philosophy*, 104.

50 See Dave Messing, "Critical Theory as Theoretical Practice: Althusserianism in Laruelle and Adorno," in *Superpositions: Laruelle and the Humanities*, eds. Rocco Gangle and Julius Greve (London: Rowman and Littlefield, 2017).

51 Laruelle, *Introduction to Non-Marxism*, 1.

52 Ibid., 11.

53 Ibid.

54 Ibid.

55 Ibid., 13.

56 Ibid., 15.

57 Ibid., 173.

58 Ibid.

59 Ibid.

60 Ibid., 173–174.

61 Ibid., 174.

62 Ibid., 11.

Chapter 5

1   I have published a version of this essay in *Postmodern Culture*. See Jonathan Fardy, "Fictionalizing Marx or Towards Non-Dialectics," *Postmodern Culture* (Vol. 30, No. 3), May 2020 (published online): https://muse.jhu.edu/article/776601.

2   Fredric Jameson, *Valences of the Dialectic* (New York: Verso, 2009), 3.

3   Ibid., 49.

4   Ibid., 50.

5   Laruelle, *Principles of Non-Philosophy*, 8.

6   Ian James, *The New French Philosophy* (Cambridge: Polity Press, 2012), 169.

7   François Laruelle, *Philosophy and Non-Philosophy*, trans. Taylor Adkins (Minneapolis: Univocal Publishing, 2013), 239.

8   Mullarkey, *Post-Continental Philosophy*, 146.

9   Smith, *Laruelle*, 119.

10 Ibid., 119–120.

11 Peter Hallward, *Badiou: A Subject to Truth* (Minneapolis: University of Minnesota Press, 2003), 25.

12 Ibid.

13 Laruelle, *Anti-Badiou*, xxxvi.

14 Ibid., xxxix.

15 Ibid., xxxi–xxxii.

16 Ibid., xxxii–xxxiii.

17 Ibid., xxxix.

18 O'Maoilearca, *All Thoughts Are Equal*, 99.

19 Jean Baudrillard, *The Perfect Crime*, trans. Chris Turner (New York: Verso, 1996), 5.

20 Ibid., 96.

21 Ibid.

22 Salvatore Mele and Mark Titmarsh, "Interview with Baudrillard," in *Baudrillard Live: Selected Interviews*, ed. Mike Gane (London: Routledge, 1993), 82.

23 Mike Gane, *Baudrillard's Bestiary: Baudrillard and Culture* (London: Routledge, 1991), 157.

24 Jean Baudrillard, *For a Critique of the Political Economy of the Sign*, trans. Charles Levin (New York: Verso, 2019), 113.

25 Ibid., 115.

26 Ibid., 114.

27 Ibid.

28 Jean-François Lyotard, *Libidinal Economy*, trans. Iain Hamilton Grant (London: Bloomsbury Academic, 2004), 116.

29 Ibid., 116–117.

30 Ibid., 119.

31 See Geoff Bennington, *Lyotard: Writing the Event* (New York: Columbia University Press, 1988).

32 Ibid., 34–35.

33 Jean Baudrillard, *The Mirror of Production*, trans. Mark Poster (New York: Telos Press, 1975), 1.

34 Ibid.

35 Ibid., 20.

36 Mike Gane, *Baudrillard: Critical and Fatal Theory* (London: Routledge, 1991), 98–99.

37 Ibid., 97.

38 Ibid., 94.

39 Baudrillard, *The Mirror of Production*, 31.

40 Ibid., 43.

41 Ibid., 98.

42 Douglas Kellner, *Jean Baudrillard: From Marxism to Postmodernism and Beyond* (Stanford: Stanford University Press, 1989), 132.

43 Ibid.

44 Jean Baudrillard, *Forget Foucault* (New York: Semiotext(e), 1987), 25.

45 Jean Baudrillard, "Why Theory?" in *Hatred of Capitalism*, eds. Chris Krauss and Sylvère Lotringer (New York: Semiotext(e), 2001), 129.

46 Jean Baudrillard, "From Radical Incertitude, or Thought as Imposter," in *French Theory in America*, eds. Sylvère Lotringer and Sande Cohen (London: Routledge, 2001), 129.

47 Ibid.

48 Ibid.

49 Laruelle, *Introduction to Non-Marxism*, 34.

50 Laruelle, *Photo-Fiction*, 62.

51 Galloway, *Laruelle*, 117.

52 Laruelle, *Photo-Fiction*, 62–63.

53 Ibid., 63.

54 Smith, *Laruelle*, 120.

55 Laruelle, *Introduction to Non-Marxism*, 1.

56 Ibid., 11.

57 Ibid., 1.

58 Ibid., 3.

59 Laruelle, *Photo-Fiction*, 9.

60. Ibid., 25.
61. Claude Lévi-Strauss, *Myth and Meaning: Cracking the Code of Culture* (New York: Schocken Books, 1979), 8.
62. Claude Lévi-Strauss, "The Structural Study of Myth," *The Journal of American Folklore* (Vol. 68, No. 270), 1955: 443.
63. Laruelle, *Photo-Fiction*, 15.
64. Ibid., 58.
65. Laruelle, *Introduction to Non-Marxism*, 91.
66. Ibid., 81.
67. Ibid., 80.
68. Francois Laruelle, "Marx with Plank," trans. Rocco Gangle in *Superpositions*, 163–164.
69. Kolozova, *Capitalism's Holocaust of Animals*, 5.
70. Ibid., 12–13.
71. Ibid., 46.
72. Ibid., 6.

Chapter 6

1. Marx, *Theses on Feuerbach*, 197.
2. Kolozova, *Capitalism's Holocaust of Animals*, 9.
3. Marx, *Economic and Philosophic Manuscripts of 1844*, 65.
4. Katerina Kolozova, *Toward a Metaphysics of Socialism: Marx and Laruelle* (Brooklyn: Punctum Books, 2015), 2.
5. Kolozova, *Capitalism's Holocaust of Animals*, 29.
6. Ibid.
7. I think it is worth noting here that it was Georg Lukács who was the first to crystallize this insight into the capitalist reduction of diverse processes to atomized things via his theory of "reification" (literally "thingification").

See Georg Lukács, *History and Class Consciousness: Studies in Marxist Dialectics*, trans. Rodney Livingstone (Cambridge: MIT Press, 1986).

8   Kolozova, *Capitalism's Holocaust of Animals*, 37.

9   Ibid., 38.

10 Ibid.

11 Ibid.

12 Ibid., 32.

13 Ibid.

14 Ibid., 37.

15 Ibid.

16 Ibid.

17 Ibid.

18 Ibid., 45.

19 Ibid., 46.

20 Kolozova, *Toward a Metaphysics of Socialism*, 42.

21 Ibid.

22 Ibid., 43.

23 Ibid., 44.

24 Ibid.

25 Ibid., 18.

26 Ibid. The phrase-concept is used throughout.

27 See Katerina Kolozova, *Cut of the Real: Subjectivity in Poststructuralist Philosophy* (New York: Columbia University Press, 2014).

28 It should be noted that Kolozova also draws upon raw material taken from Jacques Lacan for whom the Real can traumatically touch and scar the subject.

29 Kolozova, *Capitalism's Holocaust of Animals*, 4–5.

30 Ibid., 39.

31 See Jean Baudrillard, *Impossible Exchange*, trans. Chris Turner (London: Verso, 2001).

32 Henry, *Marx*, 12.

33 Kolozova, *Capitalism's Holocaust of Animals*, 56.

34 Ibid., 58.

35 Ibid.

36 Ibid.

37 Ibid., 56.

38 Ibid., 61.

39 Ibid.

40 Ibid.

41 Ibid., 56.

42 Ibid., 58.

43 Ibid.

44 Ibid., 59.

45 Ibid., 42.

46 See Donna Haraway, *Simians, Cyborgs, and Women: The Reinvention of Nature* (New York: Routledge, 1991).

47 Kolozova, *Toward a Metaphysics of Socialism*, 91.

48 Ibid., 58.

49 Ibid., 60.

50 Ibid., 87–88.

51 Ibid., 31.

52 Ibid., 33.

53 Ibid.

54 Kolozova, *Capitalism's Holocaust of Animals*, 45.

55 Ibid.

56 Kolozova, *Toward a Metaphysics of Socialism*, 38.

57 Rocco Gangle, *Diagrammatic Immanence: Category Theory and Philosophy* (Edinburgh: Edinburgh University Press, 2016), Kindle Edition, Loc. 122.

58 Ibid., 124.

59 Kolozova, *Capitalism's Holocaust of Animals*, 45.

60 Kolozova, *Toward a Metaphysics of Socialism*, 33.

61 Ibid.

Chapter 7

1 I am taking this idea of theory as a medium from W.J.T. Mitchell. See W.J.T. Mitchell, *What Do Pictures Want?: The Lives and Loves of Images* (Chicago: The University of Chicago Press, 2005).

2 Althusser, *Reading Capital*, 297.

INDEX

Locators followed by "n." indicate endnotes

"absolute" (Hegel) 2, 114, 116
Adorno, Theodor 12, 29, 197. *See also* negative dialectics
    administered life 108, 110, 116
    Aesthetic Theory 111, 113
    criticism at that virtue 117, 120
    Dialectic of Enlightenment 108
    disenchantment of the concept 9–11, 117–20
    exile and style 108–14
    identity thinking 115, 119
    Minima Moralia 108–9
    Negative Dialectics 9, 13, 109, 113, 116–17, 119–20
    nonidentity 108, 110, 112, 115, 119
aesthetic(s)
    philosophical 42–7, 161
    power of nonidentity 112
    solutions 153
Althusser, Louis 2–3, 12–13, 21–2, 35, 49, 73, 151, 154, 156, 199
    anti-humanist critique 22–4, 36, 52, 97
    class struggle 57, 60
    concepts 50
    critics 54–7
    epistemological break 50
    labor, value 50–1
    Lenin and Philosophy 58
    For Marx 50
    materialist tendency 60, 62
    overdetermination 3, 50
    partisanship in philosophy 61
    primacy/theory of theoretical practice 50, 52–4, 57, 66, 92–3, 196 (*see also* theoreticism (Althusser))
    Reading Capital 50
    symptomatic reading 50
    theoretical anti-humanism 50
    theoreticist deviation 56–8
    young Marx 50
Althusserianism 50, 55, 60–1, 73
    ideology of 55
    silence of unprovability 61
atonal music 110
autonomy of political practice 68–72, 74

Badiou, Alain 61–2, 136, 140
    Maoism 84
    philosophy, fictionalization 137–8, 141
    Philosophy for Militants 62–3
    thinkability of politics 62
Balibar, Étienne 30, 35, 66, 72
Barthes, Roland 97
Bataille, Georges 145
Baudrillard, Jean 12, 131, 133, 142–3, 146, 176, 198
    For a Critique of the Political Economy of the Sign 143–5, 149
    Forget Foucault 152–3
    impossible exchange 166
    The Mirror of Production 149–52
    symbolic exchange 147–8
    theory-fiction 14, 143, 147, 153–4, 164–7
"Being" (Heidegger) 2

Benjamin, Walter, *The Origin of German Tragic Drama* 9
Bennington, Geoff 148
Benton, Ted 60
bourgeois philosophy 22, 110
Buck-Morss, Susan 110

capitalism, philosophy and 6-7, 12, 15, 68, 75-9, 81, 101-2, 120, 123, 146, 166, 172-3, 176, 188, 195, 197
   human sciences 82
   real-abstraction 74, 76
   structural symmetry/isomorphic 77-8
capital-world 78, 81-3, 91-2, 101
chief defect 29, 170-1
class and political consciousness 71, 79
classical political economy 20, 50-1, 150-1
class struggle 54, 57-8, 60-1, 63-4, 69, 81, 99
"cogito" (Descartes) 2
commodity-fetishism 150
conceptual dictatorship of proletariat 57
constellation as method 9-12, 195. *See also specific constellations*
   fiction 11-14, 131, 135, 137-8, 158-64, 195, 198
   impossibilization 2, 11, 13, 95, 123-30, 195
   metaphysics 12, 14, 96, 169, 173-94, 195, 198
   stranger 11, 13, 20-1, 28, 90-1, 130, 189-90, 195
   struggle 11, 13, 49, 57-62, 70-1, 80, 83, 197
Critical Theory 108
"cyborg," theory 185

Deleuze, Gilles 2, 150, 152. *See also* plane of immanence
"democracy of thought" 37-8, 56, 199
Derrida, Jacques 91
   "*différance*" 2
Descombes, Vincent 97-9, 197. *See also* structuralism
dialectical materialism 36, 58, 72, 85, 144, 170
dialectics/dialectical theory 131-3, 146, 149
   certain form of thought 142-3
   identity, rule of 118
   of theory and practice 114, 149
doing theory 14, 199
Dosse, François 207 n.3
dualysis 107, 166, 186
dyadic self 169, 184-6

economism 3
Elliott, Gregory 58
   The novelty of dialectical materialism 36
Engels, Friedrich 2-3, 59, 139
   Communist Manifesto 91
   The German Ideology 28
epoché (Husserlian) 137
equivalence 2, 6-7, 12-14, 38, 41, 45, 77-80, 83, 89-90, 122-4, 155-6, 166, 174, 180, 195, 198
"essence of Man," concept. *See* "man's essence," concept of
estrangement/estrange philosophy 11-13, 15, 19, 21-8, 40, 46, 173, 189-90, 194, 196, 198
   sensuous human activity 171
   subjectification process 191
exchange 2, 6-7, 12-14, 37-8, 41, 45, 77-80, 83, 89-90, 102, 122-4, 155-6, 166, 173-4, 180, 195, 198

exchange value system 118–19,
    144–5, 150, 173

factory production 64–6
Farris, Sara 68–9
Feuerbach, Ludwig 28–9, 34–5, 140,
    170
fiction/fictionalization 11–14, 131,
    135, 195, 198. *See also* philo-
    fiction; theory-fiction
    of Badiou 137–8, 141
    matrix of 158–64, 166
    strategies of 135, 138, 143, 153
financial crash (2008) 176–7
"finite individual," concept of 26–8,
    40, 95, 102–8, 113, 196
    Philosophical Decision and 107–8
    transcendence 106
formalism 5, 183
formalization 169, 181–4
"Forms" (Plato) 2
Foucault, Michel 103, 152
    The Order of Things 104
Freudo-Marxism 147, 149

Galloway, Alexander 78, 155
Gane, Mike 143, 150–1
Gangle, Rocco 5–6, 192
    Diagrammatic Immanence 192–3
"general intellect" 189
generalized political economy 145
generic human 75–80, 191
genuine thought 62
German criticism, ideology 28–9, 31
Guattari, Félix 2, 150. *See also* plane
    of immanence

Hallward, Peter 136–7
Haraway, Donna 185
Heidegger, Martin 84–5, 140. *See also*
    "Being" (Heidegger)

Heisenberg, Werner 159
Henry, Michel 12, 15, 24–6, 35–6,
    39, 104, 180–1. *See also*
    "individual," concept
    Introduction to Marx 105
    phenomenology 39, 105–6, 179
historical materialism 36, 60, 68, 99,
    101, 170
Horkheimer, Max, *Dialectic of
    Enlightenment* 108
Hullot-Kentor, Robert 112–13

immanent metaphysics 192–3
impossibilization 2, 11, 13, 95, 123,
    195
    Marxism, failure 125–30
    non-Marxism 124
    socialist demand 124–5
"individual," concept 13, 24–5, 36, 39,
    51, 105, 110, 113

James, Ian 96
    The New French Philosophy 134
James, William 17–18
Jameson, Fredric 118–19
    Valences of the Dialectics 131–3
Jay, Martin 110

Kellner, Douglas 152
knowledge production 38, 46, 79, 138
Kolozova, Katerina 12, 19, 46, 75–6,
    82, 102, 165, 169–71, 214 n.28
    capitalism 76, 102, 177
    critical resistance 172, 184
    "the *diktat* of the real" 20, 166
    estrangement 189–90
    post-philosophical language 182
    sacrifice and martyrdom 186–9
    theory of cyborg selfhood 185–6
Kolozovan variant 12, 14, 169, 178,
    184, 198

critique of speculation 176–8
dyadic self 184–6
formalization 181–4
instances of the real 173, 178–81, 186
language as automaton 173–6, 184
physicality 169–73
radical metaphysics 169, 189–94

Labica, Georges 12, 31–5
labor power 50–1, 64–5, 70, 80–2, 150–1
Lacan, Jacques 179, 214 n.28
language as automaton 169, 173–6, 183–7
Laruelle, François 1, 3, 7, 10, 12, 14, 15–16, 20, 26, 36–7, 47, 53, 67–8, 74, 77–8, 99, 120–1, 123, 133, 179–80, 198. *See also* non-Marxism; non-philosophy/non-standard philosophy
  Anti-Badiou: On the Introduction of Maoism into Philosophy 137, 139–40
  "being-photo of the photo" 44
  A Biography of Ordinary Man 26–7, 103
  clones/cloning 5, 11, 13, 15, 21, 26, 39, 95, 135, 154, 182 (*see also specific Laruelle's concepts*)
  The Concept of Non-Photography 43–4
  critique of abstraction 102, 106
  general theory of victims 86
  Introduction to Non-Marxism 8–9, 124, 156–8
  "Marx and Plank" 163–4
  multiplicity of Marxisms 7, 163
  non-analysis 143, 190
  non-proletariat 13, 40–1, 67, 81, 83
  ontology of difference 163
  philo-fiction 14, 162, 164–7
  Philosophical Decision on the Real 2, 133
  Philosophy and Non-Philosophy 135
  Photo-Fiction 161
  pluralism of Marx's work 8
  post-Marxist intellectuals 125
  "posture" in thought 18–19, 166
  Principle of Standard Philosophy 2, 156
  Principle of Sufficient Marxism 41
  Principles of Non-Philosophy 133–4
  style of philosophy 6
  theoretical system of Marxism 53–4
  Theory of Identities 49
"the-last-instance," concept 2–3, 13, 19, 37–8, 60, 74, 134–5, 177, 199
Lenin, Vladimir 58, 69, 157
  Materialism and Empirio-criticism 58
  quite different practice of philosophy 59
Lévi-Strauss, Claude 160, 162, 165
  "The Structural Study of Myth" 160–1
Lukács, Georg 70–1, 76, 213 n.7
Lyotard, Jean-François 146, 150, 152
  Libidinal Economy 146–7, 149
  objection 147–9

Malevich, Kazimir 112
"man's essence," concept of 22–5, 105
Marx, Karl 2–3, 7, 12, 20, 25, 41, 70–1, 79, 123, 147, 152, 163, 169, 192, 195–6

INDEX

Capital 33, 36, 50, 68, 100
class and class struggle 63–4
Communist Manifesto 91
The German Ideology 28, 31, 33, 36
industrial capitalism 76, 128
language of life 82
1844 Manuscripts 21–4, 35, 171 (*see also* estrangement/estrange philosophy)
materialism 170–1
mature science 52–3
The Poverty of Philosophy 31, 33, 139–41
science of history 151, 154–5
sojourn in philosophy 28–36, 47, 195, 199
Theses on Feuerbach 29–30, 31, 33, 139, 170
today 72–3
"use-value" 145
Marxism 36, 40–1, 46, 77, 105, 122, 136, 151, 162–4, 170. *See also* non-Marxism
autonomy of politics 68–72
"clandestine" 90–1
as deficient organization 7
failure of 8, 11, 125–30, 157–8 (*see also* impossibilization)
inter-vention 42
Marxist edifice, fragmentation 7
non-Marxist practice of 47, 89, 92–3, 129, 158
philosophical judgment, totalizing 126, 128
philosophical problem 7, 100
"Marxism-fiction" 164
materialism 29, 68, 170–1, 177
dialectical 36, 58, 72, 85, 144, 170
historical 36, 60, 68, 99, 101, 170
idealism and, struggle 58–62, 70–1

matrix (of fiction) 158–64
art-thought 159, 161
Laruelle and Baudrillard 162, 164–7
matrix mechanics 159
quantum language 164
superposition 159, 161–2
Messing, Dave 122
"metaphysical exile" 109
metaphysics 12, 14, 96, 169, 195, 198. *See also* Kolozovan variant
dyadic self 169, 184–6
formalization 169, 181–4
instances of the real 173, 178–81, 186
language as automaton 173–6, 184
physicality 169–73
radical 169, 189–94
modernity 118
Money-Commodity-Money (M-C-M) 174
Money-Money prime (M-M') 174

necessity of philosophy 31, 35, 47, 117, 120
negative dialectics 95, 107–8, 114–17, 197
nonidentity thinking 115, 119
non-philosophy and 108, 120–3, 197
in practice 115
non-capitalist theory, modes of 79–80
non-dialectics 131
non-Marxism 1, 6–8, 12, 28, 37–8, 41, 46, 100, 154, 163, 198
conceptual raw materials 7
de jure 39
introduction 8–9, 156–8
object of 42, 77–8, 101
philosophically impoverish Marxism 8–9, 189

primacy, question of 92–3
struggle in 11, 13, 49, 78, 81, 84, 87, 91, 124, 158
theory practice 53, 88–92
non-Marxist praxis 80–3
non-philosophizes philosophy 142
non-philosophy/non-standard philosophy 1, 28, 37, 49, 82, 96, 107, 135–6, 200 n.1. *See also* "Real"
  aesthetics of writing 45
  basics of 1–9
  dualistic inheritance 6
  formalism 5
  immanent approach 19
  matrix 38 (*see also* matrix (of fiction))
  negative dialectics and 108, 120–3, 197
  philosophical materials 5–6, 10–11, 49, 121, 135
  physical process 18–19
  standard Marxism and 95
  structuralism and 97–8, 197
non-photography, theory of 43–4
non-standard Marxism 1, 91, 95, 108, 124
"noumena" (Kant) 2

objectification of labor 23, 171–2
object of contemplation 29, 170–1
O'Maoilearca, John 6, 15–17, 19, 37, 44–5, 135, 141, 189. *See also* thought control
organization of political practice 66
overdetermination 3, 50

philo-fiction 14, 131, 135–6, 143, 154–6, 161, 164, 167
Philosophical Decision 1–3, 8, 13, 16–17, 21, 60–1, 80–2, 88–9, 121, 140, 194, 197

empirical-transcendental doublet 158
failure of Marxism 128–9, 158
finite individual and 107–8
philosophically premised 146
as structuralist judgment 96–102
philosophically unity 56, 163
philosophical materialism (Marx) 29, 170
philosophies in person 152
philosophy. *See also* non-philosophy/non-standard philosophy; standard philosophy
  and capitalism 6–7, 12, 15, 68, 75–9, 81–2, 101–2, 120, 123, 146, 166, 172–3, 176, 188, 195, 197
  as conceptual economy 37, 79
  of economics 35
  exit from 30, 35, 42–3, 123, 195–6, 199
  Marx's sojourn in 28–36, 47, 195, 199
  necessity of 31, 35, 47, 117, 120
  in person 139–41
  and politics 57–8
  as raw materials 5, 10–11, 38, 45–6, 92, 100, 135, 137, 155, 172, 186–7
  science and 53–4, 56
  self-enveloped universe 174
  and theory 49
  transcendental material 175
physicality 169–73, 175, 191, 193
  abstract value and 172
  automaton of language and 184–5
  destruction of 176
  human sensuous activity 171
  as instance of the real 171, 178
  qua 179–80, 194, 198
plane of immanence 2
political abstractions, persons as 85

political economy, critique of 22, 33, 41, 144–5, 147, 150–1
political intervention in theory 58
political practices 62–3, 90
    anti-capitalist struggle 63
    autonomous modes 68–72, 74
    organization of 66
    primacy of 50, 92–3
    proletarianizing 71–2
    thinkability 62
post-Marxism (Lyotard) 146–7
poststructuralism 97, 175
practical force 80–1
practice of philosophizing 58–9
principle of sufficient philosophy 2, 10, 31, 41, 136, 155
Proudhon, Pierre-Joseph 33–5, 140

quantum language 164
quantum structuralization of philosophy 163
qua (standard philosophy) 4, 11, 16–17, 19, 24–5, 41, 43–4, 56, 75, 95, 107, 119, 129, 131, 179–80, 194, 197–8

radical metaphysics 169, 189–94
Rancière, Jacques, *Althusser's Lesson* 55–6
"Real" 1–3, 12, 37, 40–1, 78, 133–46
    algebraic sign 5–6
    axiomatization 3–4, 88
    concept and 10–11, 95–6, 110
    decisions on 96, 99, 135, 196
    disappearance of 142, 153
    "force-(of)-thought" 37–40, 80, 183
    foreclosure 3, 14, 21, 38–9, 81
    instances of 173, 178–81, 186
    invariant structure/gesture 96, 99, 160
    in the last instance 3, 13, 19, 74, 80, 83, 88, 93, 128, 134–5, 165, 170, 183, 188, 197
    nonconceptuality 29, 37, 115–17, 122–3
    One-in-One (oneness) 3–4, 6
    philosophical and capitalist forms 82
    radicality 12–13, 21, 42, 74, 77, 80, 84, 87–8, 133–4, 163, 170, 180, 183, 189
    real human 26–7, 81–2
    resistance/friction 4–5
    syntax of 82, 124, 182–3
    theoretical indifference 146, 149
    transcendence 21, 134, 136, 178
    unilateral duality 3, 5, 74, 165, 167
    "Victim-in-person" and 85–7, 197
    "vision-in-One" 37–8, 88, 123
    World, image of 43, 136–7
real-abstraction 74, 76, 85
"real" economy 176–7
real individual, concept 105–6
"reification," theory 153, 155, 213 n.7

Said, Edward, *Representations of the Intellectual* 109
Schoenberg, Arnold 110
science of decision 59–63
science of philosophy 53–4, 56
"selfhood," concept of 184–6
sign exchange value, system of 144–6, 176, 178
Smith, Anthony Paul 18, 79, 90, 136, 156
socialist economy of thought 124
Sohn-Rethel, Alfred 74
speculation, critique of 176–8
Spinoza, Baruch 39
standard philosophy 1–2, 13, 38, 77–8, 84, 115, 119–20, 123, 154–6, 176–7, 194, 198

decisions on Real 96, 135
form of thinking 16
judgment on 96
of photography 43–4
Principle of Standard Philosophy 2, 156
qua "organon" 4
stranger 11, 13, 20–1, 28, 90–1, 130, 189–90, 195
stranger Marxism 13, 15, 19, 37–9, 89, 196
Stranger-subject 21, 28, 39, 40–2, 46, 89, 90–1, 196
real content of the proletariat 40
structuralism 95, 99, 160, 162, 197, 207 n.3
non-philosophy and 97–8, 197
representation/models 99, 101
struggle 11, 13, 49, 80, 83, 197
ethics of 83–7
materialism and idealism 58–62, 70–1
in non-Marxism 11, 13, 49, 78, 81, 84, 87, 91, 124, 158
practice of 49, 69, 71
theory as 49, 57–9, 90
subject-in-struggle 13, 73–5, 197
supercapitalism 7, 15, 28, 38, 67, 73–4, 78–80, 89–90, 100, 102–3, 106–7, 113, 119, 122, 129, 176, 187–8, 195, 197–8
superposition, concept of 159, 161–5

theoretical democracy 163
theoretical intervention in politics 58
theoretical science 82–3
theoretical struggle 49, 90
theoreticism (Althusser) 50–4, 72–3, 93
theoreticist deviation 57–8
theory 49, 52, 153, 186–7, 199. *See also specific theory*
as mode of production 66
philosophy and 49
and practice 88–9, 92, 143, 145, 149, 151
primacy of 50, 196
as struggle 49, 57–9, 90
of theoretical practice 52, 54, 66
theory-fiction 14, 142–3, 147, 149–54, 164, 167
thinkability of politics 62
Thompson, E.P., *The Poverty of Theory* 54
thought control 15–19
thought factory 63–7
thought-for-the-Real 2, 5, 123–4, 155. *See also* "Real"
thought production 67–8
thought-world of Marxism 42, 78, 90–1, 101–2
Tronti, Mario 13, 49, 63, 67–8, 72–3, 76. *See also* workerism (Tronti)
factory production 64–6
historical materialism 68
primacy of political practice 50, 68–9, 92–3, 196–7
Workers and Capital 63–4, 70–2

unfreedom, system 116, 118, 120, 122, 124
universal, concept of 78–9
universal capitalism 100
use value 119–20, 144–5, 150

value exchange system. *See* exchange value system
Veblen, Thorstein, *Theory of the Leisure Class* 144

"Victim-in-person" 84, 86–7
    Man-in-person and 86
    Real and 85, 197
victimology, ethics of 83–7

Weber, Max 118
whole of society 64–6
"will" (Schopenhauer) 2

workerism (Tronti) 63–6, 69–70, 72–3, 93
    class consciousness and 69–71
world, concept of 136–7
Wright, Steve 69

Young Hegelians 25, 28–9, 31–2

www.ingramcontent.com/pod-product-compliance
Lightning Source LLC
Chambersburg PA
CBHW062218300426
44115CB00012BA/2122